AFRAID
TO LIVE,
AFRAID
TO DIE

AFRAID
TO LIVE,
AFRAID
TO DIE

The story of a woman paralyzed by fear,
guilt, pills and shock treatments who
thought she was going crazy and how she
found a new way of life through the
Twelve Step program — one day at a time.

BY PAT O.

First published April, 1983.

ISBN: 0-89486-147-6

Printed in the United States of America.

CONTENTS

DEDICATION

To my husband, Jim, and my two sons, Jim and Tom, who loved
me when I was unlovable;

To my E.A. friends — who gave me hope, the feeling of
belonging, along with their never-ending love, support, and
encouragement;

To the clergymen — who listened to my Fifth Steps and took
extra time to counsel me, always accepting me no matter what
I shared, giving me the feeling of a loving and forgiving
God; and

To God as I understand Him — for giving me a second chance at
life.

ACKNOWLEDGMENTS

I would like to thank my friends Cathy, Mary Jane, Helen and Dorraine for the time they spent working on this manuscript.

An extra thanks to Cathy and Mary Jane, Cathy for her input into my early chapters, and Mary Jane for typing the manuscript.

PREFACE

When I first read Pat's book I got a lot out of it. The biggest
thing I saw was her great dedication to her spiritual quest. She
was willing to go to any lengths to get better and to get all the
help she could find.

It was twenty years ago, February 15, 1962, that I had my heart
attack and saw that I was wasting my life trying to impress
others. I said on that day that I would never again do anything I
didn't believe in. I really started my spiritual quest at that time
and have continued it to this day.

But Pat's book helped me see that there have been many times
when I haven't been willing to go to any lengths to give up my
old ideas and old ways. I find, as I look back, that there are many
periods of time when I have felt so much better than I used to
feel, that I eased off on doing my work. Pat's story helped me see
that I needed to participate more fully in my own program for
growth.

Pat's detailed and honest story of her work in Emotions
Anonymous seems to me to offer a great deal of hope to anyone
who might need the Twelve Step program of E.A. Her book gives
a precise set of directions of things she did, and that anyone can
do, when she saw her powerlessness in the face of the emotional
storms that are common to many people.

Whether or not you choose to join the organization Pat joined,
you will still get understanding as well as ideas you can use in
finding a better way of life.

I also believe Pat's book to be useful to anyone in any of the
other Twelve Step programs such as Alcoholics Anonymous,
Al-Anon, Overeaters Anonymous, Gamblers Anonymous and
many others because there is a strong emotional component to all
those problems.

It has been an honor for me to know Pat, to be her friend and to watch her work her program. She reminds me of a T-shirt slogan I once saw: I ain't perfect — but parts of me are great.

Jess Lair
Bozeman, Montana
1982

CHAPTER ONE

Impression without expression
leaves depression

My name is Pat. I'm powerless over my emotions. What I really am is a neurotic who has been hospitalized, given shock treatment, and pumped full of tranquilizers and antidepressants. Then I found Emotions Anonymous. It was April of 1969. I wish I had marked that day on my calendar as it came to be the turning point of my life.

I arrived at the meeting with Ray, a neighbor who had been attending E.A. He introduced me to a woman who welcomed me with warmth and friendliness. Everything was foreign to me, and I felt skeptical and intimidated. I had second thoughts like, "Why am I here? This couldn't possibly help me with my unique problems."

The meeting began with the Serenity Prayer:

God grant me the serenity
To accept the things
I cannot change,
Courage to change the things I can,
And the wisdom to know the difference.

Then someone read the Twelve Steps of Emotions Anonymous.*

1. We admitted we were powerless over our emotions — that our lives had become unmanageable.

---

*Reprinted with permission of Emotions Anonymous, St. Paul, MN. 55104. Adapted from the Twelve Steps of *Alcoholics Anonymous*, published by A.A. World Services, New York, NY.

2. Came to believe that a Power greater than ourselves could restore us to sanity.
3. Made a decision to turn our will and our lives over to the care of God *as we understood Him.*
4. Made a searching and fearless moral inventory of ourselves.
5. Admitted to God, to ourselves, and to another human being the exact nature of our wrongs.
6. Were entirely ready to have God remove all these defects of character.
7. Humbly asked Him to remove our shortcomings.
8. Made a list of all persons we had harmed, and became willing to make amends to them all.
9. Made direct amends to such people wherever possible, except when to do so would injure them or others.
10. Continued to take personal inventory and when we were wrong, promptly admitted it.
11. Sought through prayer and meditation to improve our conscious contact with God *as we understood Him,* praying only for knowledge of His will for us and the power to carry that out.
12. Having had a spiritual awakening as the result of these Steps we tried to carry this message, and to practice these principles in all our affairs.

I looked at the Twelve Steps critically. "How can *that* help me? And what is all this God stuff?" Seeing God mentioned in so many of the Steps, I was fearful of what this program and group were all about. I sat quietly and listened to the people talking about their experiences and their feelings. I sat silent, afraid I'd make a mistake and say the wrong thing.

Initially, I felt different from the others, but as I continued listening I heard some things I could identify with. Some of these people, too, had been hospitalized, undergone shock treatments, took different kinds of drugs, and had suicidal tendencies. Their feelings of inadequacy, failure, loneliness and desperation hit home. Never before had I heard anyone share those kinds of experiences and feelings.

Hope glimmered slightly, and I wondered what *they* could do for me. I was not yet aware of the intense discipline *I* would have to exercise if I wanted to become well. No one was there to "fix" me. They were there to support and encourage me. Someone suggested that I should come back to meetings for three months, and if I did not like what I had received at that point, the group would refund my misery. What did I have to lose by trying? My time had no value when I felt so miserable and worn out. So I came back.

At Emotions Anonymous I learned that *not* dealing with emotions can cause nervousness and other such manifestations of panic, anxiety, abnormal fear, guilt, tension, loneliness, self-pity, remorse, worry, boredom, indecision, withdrawal, fatigue, despair, and insomnia. Further suppression of emotions can lead to paranoia, compulsive behavior, obsessive thoughts, scrupulosity, suicidal and homocidal tendencies, psychosomatic and physical illnesses. Emotions which are controlled, repressed, and denied cause our minds and bodies to react. That was a scary idea for me to handle because I believed feelings such as anger, jealousy, envy and revenge were sinful. Because of the way I saw sin, it was extremely hard for me to begin to look at myself.

The disciplines of the program were difficult that first year. It is hard to understand why I fought the program the way I did. I thought no one could possibly *want* to stay sick. Then I began to realize that if I stayed sick, I was miserable, but at least I knew how to handle it, and no one expected anything from me. On the other hand, getting well meant taking responsibility for myself and not being able to blame others or my background for the way I was. I was scared. Maybe I might not actually be able to get well.

Around that time, I heard of a clergyman named Phil Hansen who talked once a week to the chemically dependent patients at a treatment center in Minnesota. I attended one of his lectures, and it helped me understand myself. I identified with the escapism of alcoholism. I had turned to pills to escape reality.

Rev. Hansen drew a box on the blackboard to represent the human mind. The subconscious makes up the greatest part of it and everything we learn since birth is retained there, he said. In addition to normal, everyday things, our subconscious mind also retains the values and attitudes we learn while growing up. He pointed out how the subconscious part always tries in one way or another, to go back to past ways of dealing with life. That is the enormity of the illness. Another name for it is rationalization, which means to find illogical, not reasonable, reasons to support unreasonable behavior.

This had become my pattern for living. Is it any wonder that when the conscious mind said, "I want to get well; I cannot stand living this way any longer. This way of life is slowly killing me," my subconscious mind answered with its learned, inadequate way of responding by saying, "You have taught me everything I know. Now you want me to change? Forget it. It is too scary, too risky."

Across the box drawn on the board Hansen wrote the letters A.A. for Alcoholics Anonymous, the most successful program for this illness. Mentally I substituted E.A. He said, "Make a commitment. Go to your meetings, read your *Twenty-Four Hours a Day* book,* and find a Higher Power. Decide this now. Don't wait for another day and wonder if you should go."

I wanted to be well more than I wanted to stay sick, but there were many times when I would think, "I wonder if I am really powerless over my emotions. I don't think I really need to go to a meeting every week. I have learned enough, now I can do it on my own. I don't think this E.A. is helping me. I am unique, my symptoms are unique, my problems are different. I can't cope. Those people wouldn't like me if they really knew me. They will judge me or criticize me. I don't want to open up to strangers. I see other sick people and they don't go to meetings, so why should I? I'm too busy to go, I am tired of all this repetition and discipline." Luckily, I recognized this kind of thinking as rationalization. It was an attempt to go back to my old ways.

"Impression without expression leaves depression," said Rev. Hansen. Even as a small child, I remembered being very impressionable. I could see that my denying and burying painful experiences had resulted in not only depression, but in all the other manifestations of such an illness.

Accepting how important the meetings and being honest were to my staying well, I kept going back to meetings. As I started to share some of my feelings in the group, oftentimes I cried. I

---

*Published by Hazelden Educational Materials.

hated my tears because I had always felt crying was stupid or childish. The people in the group reassured me that many of them had cried, too. What a relief not to be put down, but to feel understood and accepted! At first I went to my meetings because I felt I had to, but after a few months, I went because I wanted to. Being powerless over my emotions meant I could not control them. I was helpless to do it on my own, because I was not self-sufficient. As time passed, I found it was much easier to *admit* my powerlessness than to actually *accept* it.

I had stopped wanting to be myself at a very early age because I felt others did not like the real me. Through E.A., however, I came to realize that even if someone did not accept me, that did not mean I was not okay. This was a totally new way of looking at life, because I had always let other people's reactions affect my feelings of worth. When I put myself into a mold I thought others would find acceptable, I lost touch with myself. I was shocked to find I had given up my whole identity in an effort to find acceptance.

So who was the real me? Discovering myself was a slow, exciting, scary and painful process. As I kept coming back to meetings, the acceptance I felt from the group showed me I was not alone. There were other people with feelings just like mine. Finally, I felt I belonged somewhere, and I felt at home. For the next several months I was on a tremendous high, I had found hope! My energy, which had almost gone, came surging back. For the first time, I started to feel there just might be some purpose for my life.

Accepting myself as the First Step of E.A. talks about, freed me to become more healthy and responsible. This Step says that because we are powerless and our lives are unmanageable, we cannot do it alone. We need others, and we need a Higher Power to help us. If I had the power to change myself, I surely would have done so before. By no act of willpower was I able to change my destructive ways. The paradox of my illness was that the harder I tried, the more out of control I actually became. A part of me rebelled against the fact that my life was out of control and that I could not change on my own. I thought I was supposed to be strong and self-sufficient, and I saw unmanageability as weakness. When I was able to start accepting my unmanageability and my weakness, strength emerged that I never realized I had.

I met Jess Lair, a psychologist and author, at a time when I was not able to accept myself with the feelings I was acknowledging through my exposure to E.A. His understanding and total acceptance of my feelings helped me to keep going forward when I felt overwhelmed and wanted to quit trying. I agreed with most of the things Jess shared with me, but one insight was quite upsetting. "A neurotic is someone who is never pleased with anything." Although I knew he was speaking generally and not specifically to me, I took it to heart and went home and cried the rest of the day. I thought, "God, I do not want to be this way the rest of my life." Seeing my eyes swollen and red, my eleven-year-old son Jim asked, "Mom, why have you been crying all day?" I told him what Jess had said. Jim replied, "Mom, I think you're okay." His acceptance really helped. It made me remember that I only have to accept my neurosis one day at a time, just like the alcoholic accepts alcoholism one day at a time. In admitting and accepting my neurosis, I was starting to find a meaning to my life.

I used to fear that if I acknowledged a particular feeling, I would automatically act on it. The feeling would take control of me. How totally opposite reality is. I learned that when we acknowledge our feelings, we are able to make a choice to act or not to act. When we deny our feelings, they take control.

CHAPTER TWO

I needed people — not pills

I have believed in God since early childhood. I was raised Roman Catholic and took my religious practices and rituals very seriously. Too seriously! I recall being told that God was a record-keeper of everything I had done wrong. For my wrongs, I would have to perform acts of penance if I was ever going to make it to heaven. If something seemingly bad happened to me, I felt I was being punished. I thought the only people good enough for God's acceptance were the clergy.

I was a very impressionable child, and I knew my mother would be extremely proud if any of her children were to go into the religious life. So, at the age of seven, I used to parade around at home with a blanket on my head, pretending I was a nun in a classroom. Then I had a horrifying experience with my teacher in third grade. She accused me of showing my underpants to the boys by the manner in which I was sitting. She took me aside, pulled my underpants down, and spanked me. I felt humiliated. It was devastating for me because I did not feel I had done what she said, but because the teacher was a nun, part of me believed it. A couple of years later, another nun told me when I turned around in the pew at church I looked like an owl. I had just gotten my first pair of glasses and was thrilled to be able to see. Being told I looked like an owl was embarrassing, and I felt ugly.

Those experiences, along with a few more involving religion, contributed to my feeling more and more frightened of God. I thought priests and nuns dropped directly from heaven. When criticized by them, I felt rejected by God. I told these experiences to no one. I thought if I told anyone they would blame me as well, so I repressed them and tried harder to be good.

I was the youngest of twelve children, and when I was eleven my father died suddenly of a heart attack. To my knowledge, he had never been sick. He and my mom went to visit her parents for the day. While there, he collapsed on a chair and died instantly. When my brother-in-law came to tell us about Dad, he said, "Pa died." My reaction was, "You do not mean Pa. You mean Grandpa. Pa is too young to die at only fifty-four." He said, "No, it's Dad." I was eating a dish of ice cream, and I got a big lump in my throat and nothing more would go down. This lump in my throat stayed for several days. That night I went to bed crying my heart out and spent the night tossing and turning. I could not or would not believe Dad was really dead. My denial was very strong, and the next few days were overwhelming. Even seeing him in the casket did not make me believe. The time at the mortuary and funeral was scary, and I felt that what was happening was not real. I do not recall anyone in the family sharing their feelings. I did not even want to feel because it was too painful. I felt really lonely, but knew I would not be a "big girl" if I cried.

I was to enter the sixth grade a few days later. At the beginning of each school year we had to fill out family information. When it came to filling out my father's name, I broke down and cried. I thought it was not fair for other children to have a father and, in my childish mind, I prayed that God would send him back. When my prayers were not answered, I thought it was because I was being punished or was not worthy. Believing God was the cause of my father's death, I became so frightened of Him I tried to become even more perfect to gain His acceptance.

Shortly after my father's death, my mother had a nervous breakdown and was hospitalized. I felt even more frightened and alone. When I heard that she had been locked up after running away from the hospital I thought she was being mistreated, and I was afraid I might lose her, too. Since I believed God had caused her breakdown, my fear of Him increased. If only someone who loved me had sat down with me and explained what was happening, I might not have been quite so frightened. Because there was no one to talk to, I pushed down the fears and hurts thinking this would make them go away. Repression was becoming a pattern in my life.

For years I tried to remember more about my relationship with my father. Others in the family spoke highly of Pa and their experiences with him. When they did, I felt left out. For some reason I do not understand, I was afraid of him.

I remember going to market with Pa a couple of times in the wee hours of the morning to sell our asparagus. I really enjoyed that. We would stop at a restaurant and have a roll and a glass of milk. There were a few times when Dad took me along as he delivered potatoes to a trucker, and on the way home we stopped to get an ice cream cone. These were times I liked being with my dad, because being alone with him made me feel special. At home I felt left out with so many others there.

Because I remembered so little of my relationship with Dad, I started to wonder if something traumatic had happened that I had blocked off. Realizing that if we block off the negative, we also end up blocking out the positive, I did some soul searching. Not coming up with any trauma in our relationship, other than that of his death, I now believe the relationship was simply what I remembered it to be. What I was really looking for by trying to remember more of a relationship were feelings of being loved by my father. When my brothers and sisters recalled their experiences with our dad, I felt he loved them and not me. Because I had so little to relate, I felt left out and unloved. I am not saying love was not there, only that I did not feel it.

In the years after my dad died, I put on a lot of weight. Eating seemed to make me feel better. Until writing this, I never realized that the eating was helping me cover my pain. Since I was overweight, I had to go to a special store to get clothes. Through the store I would get circulars in the mail saying, "LUCKY YOU! You're a chub!" I had seven older brothers, some of whom teased me. When they saw the circulars in the mail, I heard over and over again, "LUCKY YOU! You're a chub!" At that point, I did not feel good about myself, and their teasing me about my weight caused me to feel even more fat, ugly and not liked. Because I was so sensitive and reacted to almost anything, I, of course, got teased more. I was also teased about the things I did and how I acted. When I was teased, I ran to my mother, and she would stick up for me saying, "Don't pick on Patty." Today when someone calls me Patty, I get a nauseous feeling in my stomach because it reminds me of the little girl who desperately needed to grow up.

As I examined my belief in God, I found it was rigid and narrow — black was black and white was white; there were no gray areas. Knowing this rigidity had made me so sick, I had a choice. Did I still want to hang onto those beliefs, or did I want to choose to have an open mind and listen to how others had changed? At meetings I listened intently when people talked about God. I went to hear people speaking on the Twelve Steps. Along with reading E.A. literature, I started to read other books recommended by members. I literally devoured everything I heard and read like a starving person, for I had been starving — not only emotionally, but spiritually as well. It was shocking to find I could be so involved in a religious denomination and yet be spiritually bankrupt.

One night I heard Phil Hansen, sharing his concept of God, say, "You are the object of God's love. God loves you just the way you are. Don't say you have never heard it, because you heard it tonight, March 12, 1970." It touched me so deeply because I had never heard it before. Whenever I feel guilty or unworthy, I choose to remember those words. He also said, "When we get to heaven, there will be no denominations there." I was so ingrained with the idea that my religion was the only way to heaven, yet I doubted I would even make it. How wonderful to hear that God was open to all of His children no matter what their beliefs might be. How ready I was to let go of my rigid thinking, because it was destroying me. Since Rev. Hansen was of a different denomination, my willingness to be open to what he was saying was an outward sign of my decision to let go of my former thinking and beliefs.

I have heard it said in E.A., and I believe it is true, that if we did not feel love from our parents, particularly from our fathers, it makes it difficult for us to experience a loving God. Many of us who ended up in E.A. did not feel the love and acceptance of a parent who helped us realize a loving Higher Power. We can keep blaming our parents or our past for not believing in a loving God and stay locked in, or we can accept the way it was and come to find a way to change those feelings today. I recall Jess Lair saying, "For what I was in the past, shame on my parents.

But if I stay that way, shame on me." When I really wanted change, my attitudes and behavior started changing.

Because I feared rejection and pain, the scariest thing in the world for me was to reach out and trust another human being. Once I became aware that the alternative to not trusting and reaching out was actually more painful, I was willing to try. No longer could I tolerate the loneliness and isolation. I was afraid to reach out to anyone for fear they would die, they would move away, or they would no longer want to keep up a relationship. The grown-up world of reality means learning to handle these experiences and not be devastated by them.

I remember sitting in my front yard knowing I desperately needed to talk to someone in E.A. Ray and Helen lived just two doors away. Would I risk being laughed at or rejected? Although each time I took the risk I received acceptance and encouragement, I still feared ridicule. For several years, Ray and Helen had listened to me and encouraged me almost daily. I used to think, "They must be getting sick of me," yet they always welcomed me back. Helen paid me a touching compliment when she gave a talk at one of our retreats for E.A. members. She said, "My good friend, Pat, used to come over and share her pain with me, and her pain helped me to grow, too." This was great to hear because there were times I felt as if I were a burden and a pest. Ray and Helen will always have a special spot in my heart for their unending support of the overwhelming needs I had then. I am grateful to my Higher Power for putting them both into my life.

Pride was my biggest obstacle to getting the help I needed, and it can still be today, if I let it. When I did not want to reach out to someone, I would use some of these excuses: I don't want to bother them; I'll be imposing; they are too busy; I'm not important enough to take their time; they won't really understand me; they will think I am foolish or silly because I feel the way I do; I am just a burden; they must be sick of listening to me; I should be strong; I should not need people so much; or I should just need God.

A couple of verses that illustrate God touching us through people are:

"I looked for my God, He I could not see.
I looked for my soul; it eluded me.

I sought my brother; I found all three."[1]
                              and
"I sought to hear the voice of God.
I climbed the highest steeple,
God said, Come down, my child,
I dwell among the people."[2]

I honestly believe we cannot say we have a wonderful relationship with a Higher Power if we do not have a relationship with the people closest to us. Love from God extends to others. An idea from scripture that also opened my eyes was, "How can you say you love God whom you have never seen, if you do not love your brother whom you do see?" I cannot delude myself today by thinking I love God if I do not treat the people sent into my life by my Higher Power with some compassion and respect.

In the early years of E.A., before the *Emotions Anonymous* book was published, I read and re-read A.A.'s books. One of them was *Twelve Steps and Twelve Traditions*.[3] Whenever I read the chapter on Step Two, one word always stood out — defiance. Because defiance is so subtle, I did not see it on my own. It was startling and painful to believe that I actually felt defiance for God even though I tried to be good. Seeing the anger under my defiance really frightened me, because I believed anger toward God was a serious sin. I found it extremely difficult to face these feelings.

Today, when I hear myself saying, "Why me? It isn't fair; I don't need this, or, this is more than I can handle," I know defiance is back. It is healthy to question things, but refusal to accept reality will not cause reality to change and will only cause me more fear and suffering.

I had never thought to pray about what God's will was for me. Instead, I was always telling Him what I thought was best for me. I had prayed but, because I did not know how to, I had not let Him in. I needed to realize that God had not caused the painful experiences in my life. He did not want me to suffer, and He was not punishing me. He loved me and wanted only good for me.

---

[1] Author Unknown

[2] Author Unknown

[3] *Twelve Steps and Twelve Traditions*, published by A.A. World Services, Inc., New York, NY. Also available from Hazelden Educational Materials

God gives human beings a free will to choose, and it is human choices that cause most of our pain. Realizing I could not believe in His love and care and at the same time defy and question Him was a spiritual awakening I will always treasure. Trust and rebellion do not go hand in hand; believing means reliance — not defiance.

Before E.A., I felt guilty about the doubt and despair I felt. Because I thought doubt and despair were sinful, it was hard to be honest about these feelings. What I needed to do with my feelings was to talk about them and listen to how others dealt with these same emotions. Each time I faced my doubts, they not only dissipated, but I became more conscious of a loving God. I actually found answers to things I had previously been told had no answers.

Whenever new ideas for growth come to me, I still get scared. Doubt and fear can return, but the experiences of seeing the many times God has come through for me and for others in E.A. makes it a little easier to trust. It helps me to remember that God will never allow anything to happen that will destroy me or wipe me out. Today, I am grateful for the doubts that have kept me searching to understand God as a loving Higher Power. I believe this knowledge will continue as I grow. Changing my concept of God was a slow and painful process, because the old tapes of a record-keeping God were so powerful. These tapes come back again and again.

Through doubts, despair, struggles, reaching out and risking, and by being myself with people who understand, I have come to see that when I was reaching for my pills for happiness, it could never be found because love cannot come from a pill. Love is only found by being who we really are. It may sound strange, but I realize now there were some people who really cared for me in my life, but I could not accept their love because I felt they did not see the real me. They only saw the phony me who was trying to be acceptable in their eyes. I had to take responsibility for my phoniness.

Many of the people who come to E.A. are frightened by the word *sanity*, but it seemed to fit me. In E.A. I found I could keep my sanity and not end up in an institution. I was also grateful to learn that insanity was a choice. When I feared insanity for so many years, I thought it was just something that happened. I began to see that insanity came from the behavior of continually denying reality. The program promises, "No one will fail to get well who has the capacity to be honest." Oh, how I prayed to be honest. I was afraid I might not be able to be totally honest until I heard willingness was the key. Being willing seemed easy enough, and when I wasn't, all I needed to do was to pray for willingness.

In E.A. we talk more simply about sanity and insanity. Oftentimes, the insanity of the illness is simply not accepting our powerlessness over it. Isn't it a form of insanity to not want to face reality? When I think about it, aren't these behaviors and attitudes insanity?

1. I deny my real identity to gain acceptance from others.
2. I am supposed to be perfect.
3. I try to be self-sufficient.
4. I need to control.
5. If I lose control, I will go insane.
6. I look for love in a pill.
7. I turn anger, fear, and guilt in on myself.
8. I react to what others say, and I feel rejected.
9. I lash out in anger and blame others.
10. I hold resentments, re-feeling old hurts and pain.
11. I feel responsibility for others.
12. I feel guilty for no reason.
13. My problems and symptoms are unique.
14. I can change my feelings or deny them by using will power.
15. I feel unworthy, and there is no purpose to my life.

Anyone who reads my list will understand why I had no quibble with the Second Step, "Came to believe that a Power greater than ourselves could restore us to sanity."

CHAPTER THREE

Strength comes from accepting weakness

Making a decision was something I tried to avoid. A decision meant the possibility of a mistake. Mistakes meant I was wrong, wrong was a sin, and sinning was to be avoided at all costs. Sinning meant feelings of guilt, failure, and condemnation.

As far back as I can remember, I had allowed all my decisions on morality to be made by clergy. Mentally, I never weighed the possibility of the lesser of two evils. I had never heard anything about the spirit of the law. Today, I see the spirit of the law as healthier than my rigid conformity to the letter of the law.

What value is there in doing something good if we are doing it only out of fear? I had the idea that if I *thought* something was wrong, it was wrong. I saw this reasoning had to be eliminated, because I had become so scrupulous that I felt guilty about almost everything. This kind of thinking kept me so tied up I became less and less able to function. I had the underlying feeling I had committed some sin that was condemning me to hell and, for the life of me, I did not know what it was. This feeling caused me much fear and anxiety.

Relief finally came when I became aware there was nothing I had done or could ever do that would separate me from the love of God. If I was to grow up, I was going to make mistakes. Mistakes were just a reality that I was human. To learn and to grow from my mistakes was what my Higher Power wanted for me. The biggest mistake I could make would be in trying to be perfect. By trying to be perfect, I would be burying what little ability I felt I had. God gave me my humanity in order for me to relate to others.

Before Emotions Anonymous, I had never heard the word *surrender* as either a spiritual or religious idea. My initial act of surrender was something I was not consciously aware I had done. As I look back, I see it came when I was willing to give up believing I could do anything about my illness on my own. I had to throw out the old ways of dealing with life, because they had not worked.

After a while, I learned the difference between surrender and compliance. Surrender says, "I give in, I have no answers, I need help. I have not been able to do it on my own, and I need a Higher Power and other people." Compliance says, "Maybe today I cannot do it alone, I will learn a few things, I will do these things as long as the pressure is on, but there will come a day when I really won't be powerless any more, then I will be able to do it on my own." With compliance, there is a closed, egotistical and defiant attitude through which little can penetrate. Loneliness continues. With surrender, there is an openness, a willingness to trust, a change in attitude. New insights come flooding in along with a feeling of hope and belonging. I saw there could be no real change without surrender.

We all experience a fear of letting go. After falling several feet down a steep cliff, a mountain climber clung for his life to a small tree branch jutting out of the rock. While hanging on, he hollered, "Is there anybody up there who can help me?" A voice came back, "This is God. Just let go, and you'll be okay." The climber hollered back, "Is there anybody else up there?" Surrender is really safe and secure, but our reasoning often tries to tell us we need control.

Like the mountain climber, I either don't surrender until I have tried every other way I can think of, or I surrender only when my pain is so great that I must let go. I know God gave me a brain, but so often I have used it to try to intellectualize my problems and solve them entirely on my own. Oftentimes, I limit the ways in which God can work, but when I give in and say, "This situation seems hopeless; I cannot see anything more that I can do," that is when God surprises me by suddenly showing me one of His ways to help me.

In surrender, we cannot just sit back, fold our hands, and say, "God, you take over." He gave us a mind to use, and we need to do our part. When I am not trying to be perfect, I seem to know what my part is. I have heard it said in E.A., "Pray as if everything depends on God and act as if everything depends on you." When I look back at these past years and see how little I have actually surrendered, I marvel at the change my Higher Power has been able to bring about in my life. My self-will has slammed the door shut on Him many times.

Today, I see willingness as the key to surrender: a willingness to let go of the old ideas, a willingness to accept my feelings, and a willingness to trust in my Higher Power and other people. I also see that surrender must be done on a daily basis.

In the beginning, the struggle to surrender and let go of my idealism was overwhelming and scary. What could replace my idealism? I had a certain perfect picture of what I should be. Every time I saw something in myself that did not live up to this ideal, guilt took over. I had to accept before I could surrender; my guilt interfered with the process of acceptance. Over and over I needed to hear, "Accept your humanity and stop expecting perfection," and "Feelings are not moral, they are neither good nor bad in themselves."

Before Emotions Anonymous I had no idea I was such an idealist. I discovered my high ideals caused my neurotic guilt which, in turn, caused my emotional problems. I wanted success without effort, pleasure without pain, peace of mind without looking within, and perfection without recognizing my faults. I had been running away from myself, because I did not want to risk making a mistake. I had an unrealistic self-image and had become self-centered and egotistical. How rigid and immature I was. These insights were a result of hearing other E.A. members share themselves.

When I saw myself sometimes back in the driver's seat trying to control, I became frustrated. After all, I had learned I should know better. It was humbling to read in a book written by an alcoholic priest, "The saints were always surprised they did as well as they did."[4] When I think I should do better, these words help me to accept myself.

The point at which each person hits his emotional bottom is different. The people who amaze me are the ones who appear to

---

[4] *The Golden Books*, by Fr. John Doe, The SMT Guild, P.O. Box 1194, Indianapolis, IN. Also available from Hazelden Educational Materials.

be suffering and continually reject the acceptance given by the group, because they think they are unique. Or the person who repeatedly ends up in the hospital, because he refuses to trust another person or a Higher Power. They seem desperate to me, but I believe from my own experience they have not as yet hit their bottom. They won't give up their will because they still want control. They do not want anyone else running their life — not even a Higher Power. False pride is blocking their ability to surrender. Surrender and control are not compatible.

When I was new in the program, I was mainly concerned about my own recovery. My control was centered around myself, trying to get people to act the way I wanted them to and to treat me the way I wanted to be treated. After experiencing some recovery, I realized I was trying to control those close to me for their own good. This appalled me. Surrendering my own will and life was easier than letting go of my children. Now I know I can turn to my Higher Power for help. I do not know where my children are at spiritually or what belief, if any, they have in a Higher Power, but I do know my playing God in their lives will only end in frustration. My alternative is to accept that I gave them the best guidance I was able to give. Letting them go is trusting and believing that the God I have come to believe in is taking care of and guiding them. God's love finally got through to me, and it will get through to my children when they are receptive.

The reason I would like to have my children find a meaningful relationship with a Higher Power now is to keep them from going through needless suffering. Although this may sound virtuous, I know better. I see that my pride wants my children to be good reflections on me. I also see that I not only want to save them from more pain, but I want to save myself from added pain. Seeing their pain puts me in touch with my own sense of inadequacy and failure. I do not like to be reminded of how long it took me to come to terms with my own humanity. Trying to avoid pain is still very much a part of me. At least now I know pain does not come from God but is a part of living. As I face it, I develop more understanding and compassion for myself and, in turn, for others. Before my E.A. days, I was so involved in my own misery I was not capable of listening to someone else's problems.

A couple of years into the Twelve Step program I heard an A.A. member say that if he had waited to work the program until he understood God, he would be dead. He reinforced what I was learning in E.A. More recently, another alcoholic shared how his sponsor told him in his early A.A. days that he did not have to understand or even believe the program would work, and he did not have to want to come to meetings; he just had to do it. His sponsor told him to ask God for help each morning, go to a meeting each night, and thank God at the end of each day. He did this thinking, "I'll show my sponsor how their program won't work for me." After two months of "acting as if," he believed. He had a spiritual awakening. When I hear people relate experiences like these, it renews my faith in the program and helps me remember that I do not have to understand or believe in the program. Trying to understand has often hindered me from making progress.

I believe the same capacity to destroy ourselves, when it is surrendered, equals our capacity to grow, be responsible, and be more creative than we may have ever dreamed possible. Not only do I need to continue to accept my weaknesses, but I need also to be grateful for them. St. Paul put it so beautifully and simply: "When I am weak, then I am strong." When St. Paul prayed to God asking that the thorn in his side be removed, God answered, "My Grace is sufficient." When St. John ended up in prison he was disappointed that his life should end that way. Then he came to see that many people were finding God by his remaining there. I did not want to accept my pain or illness either. Although I believe God could have cured me instantly if He had willed, I think He has chosen to arrest my illness, one day at a time, so I could be an instrument of His healing and love where I am.

Gert is a striking example of this. She is a cute, little old gal in her seventies who spoke one night at an open A.A. meeting. She related how she found God. Until her mid-fifties, she had no religious background but she had money and fame. She had everything a lot of people thought should make her happy. She had gone through her third marriage and into alcoholism. Having tried unsuccessfully to take her life, she was at a point of despair. She was finally able to start accepting a Higher Power when someone gave her a concept of God she could handle. "You seem heavily burdened, maybe you could think of Him as someone to carry your baggage." Because of this love and concern, with no strings attached, Gert accepted that concept of a Higher Power and started believing. From that concept, her faith grew, and for years she traveled all over the world sharing her spiritual and religious convictions and inspiring many people. Because Gert was spiritually accepted, she became one of the greatest, most dynamic instruments of God's healing and love I have ever encountered.

If you are an atheist or an agnostic and have read this far, I hope you are not turned off. If you are, I understand. Phil Hansen was talking one night about the atheist and the agnostic and said, "An atheist believes in something and that becomes his God. The agnostic is a searcher for God." The truth is that I was more in the category of the agnostic than I cared to admit. With all my religious background, I did not even know it. In a way, I feel more comfortable when someone new comes to a meeting and says, "I don't believe in God"; or, "I don't think God is fair"; or, "I think God has forgotten me." At least these people are honest with their feelings and because of their honesty, they are open and receptive. I believe the person who comes in professing faith and talking about their wonderful relationship with God is deluded. It is hard to reach a person who already thinks he has this kind of relationship. If he truly does have all the answers, why is he coming to E.A. meetings?

Anyone who is willing to be honest and wants to get help can make a beginning by just simply believing he or she is not the center of the universe; there is something else that might help. It might be a group of people who have already found some help. I believe the care of God, as we understand Him, is put in Step Three not so that we try to analyze and understand God, but so that people can start right where they are. I do not try so hard to understand God now, because I have come to believe if I could really understand Him, I would be God.

CHAPTER FOUR

Hurt has to be looked at to be healed

The last thing I wanted to do was look back over my life. When Ray said, "Why don't you start writing down your inventory so you can do the Fourth Step?" I felt like saying, "Mind your own business and bug off." I wanted to forget my past. I had suffered pain from others and, in turn, caused others a lot of pain. Why would I want to dig up that garbage? Then I heard, "Hurt has to be looked at to be healed." If I ever wanted to function as a whole person, I would have to look at the things that bothered me from my past, the fears, the hurts, the shames, the guilts, the self-pity, and the resentments. Those experiences I was able to deal with came to my conscious mind as I prayed for the willingness to see them. I found it was important to write these experiences down. This way, when I was ready for my Fifth Step, I could not rationalize these experiences away.

I kept hearing the word *honesty*. I had always thought of myself as a fairly honest person, but the honesty they talked about here had a different slant to it — honesty to self. I could see I had not been honest where it really mattered. Fear and pride had been my biggest obstacles. When I started to look within, fear said, "You dare not look" and pride said, "You need not look." Pride and fear had to be put on the shelf.

I now see how much I picked up the negative experiences in my life. I learned to deal with fearful situations by denying them, and I learned to deal with shameful and guilt-ridden situations by repressing them. This denial and repression caused all my symptoms of emotional illness. All feelings do come out somehow.

In doing the Fourth Step inventory I saw myself as a little child: over-sensitive, fearful, and guilt-ridden. In my over-sensitivity, I reacted and felt a lot of rejection. Whether it was really rejection or not did not matter — I perceived it as such. My fears came out in many areas, but most noticeably when I was having new experiences and meeting new people. My guilt came out in situations where I could not accept my humanity. For example: About the age of five, I broke my collarbone when I fell out of a wagon. Even though I complained loudly, I was not taken to a doctor until the following day. I felt hurt because my pain was minimized.

I remember a man coming to our door and my brother telling me he was coming to pick up any little kids he found. Whenever I saw a stranger coming up our driveway, I ran and hid behind the davenport. I was teased for the fear I displayed, and this caused me to feel lonely, put down and even more afraid of the unknown. When I was old enough to realize my brother had been teasing me to get a reaction and that what he said was not true, I thought, "Adults are cruel and uncaring."

When I started school, I did not know anyone in my class. For several weeks I cried at home and at school because I did not want to go. It was very painful for me.

Throughout my childhood, fear continued to come out in various areas. I remember going to my first movie. A fire was shown on the screen, and I thought the theatre was on fire. I ended up crying in the lobby. World War II was going on during this time, and my oldest brother was in the service. My mother often talked about her fear of communism. She told me that if the communists took over the world, they would take children away from their parents. I worried a lot in my early years about being separated from my family. When I was nine years old, a sexual experience with a relative was very traumatic for me.

In remembering all of these things through the Fourth Step inventory, I relived my father's death and the traumas the nuns had caused me. I realized how childhood realities, when repressed, later become the neuroses of the adult.

As this awareness came, I was frightened of what I saw. I carried that fear around until one day I read a book by an author who shared similar feelings. He had discovered that in the depth of our being we are not bad or evil. Because we are created by God, the core of our being is good. This idea helped me lose the fear of what I still might find within myself. I knew that no matter how much garbage there might be, I was good underneath. I also realized that God would not show me any more at one time than I could handle. This gave me the courage to look back at what needed to be seen.

I had picked up the idea that sex was dirty and sinful and that "impure" thoughts were as bad as if you actually did whatever you were thinking of. If you did not entertain the temptation, then it was not a sin. Because I did not want to sin, I tried pushing any of these thoughts away. Sometimes this worked, but more often, this technique only gave my thoughts more power.

My first menstrual period was extremely frightening since no one had prepared me for this natural occurrence. Sex, or anything pertaining to it, was never mentioned in our home. From this, I perceived it must be something awful.

Entering high school, I was frightened of the unknown, and I did not want to reach out to make new friends again. Thoughts about my high school days brought memories of insecurity and pain. It was hard for me to reach out to new relationships. How lucky (now I call it the Grace of God) I was to have joined up with the close handful of friends I had. I remember, especially, a boyfriend, Ron, and I realize how fortunate I was to have cared about someone who respected me and did not take advantage of my vulnerability. I can admit today, because of a more realistic self-image, how desperately I wanted to be loved. I have gained understanding and now have compassion for the people I knew back in high school who were getting into trouble. They were not bad, they were only looking for love and acceptance.

In my senior year I met Jim, the man I eventually married. My brother was going out with his sister, and they ultimately married too. Jim and I had a stormy courtship, dating off and on for the next two years. Sometimes I wanted him around, and sometimes I wanted him to get lost. I don't know if my problem was that I could not handle someone really caring about me, or if I was afraid of letting someone get too close and my getting hurt. When we decided to get married, unfortunately, my reason for marrying Jim was not a healthy one. I had married him so I would have someone to take care of me, and because I did not think anyone else would have me.

Two months after we were married I became pregnant and suffered from morning sickness. The job I had at the time made it mandatory to quit working at the end of the seventh month. After I quit, I began to suffer from anxiety and boredom. I became a compulsive cleaner.

Our son, Jim, was born a healthy and beautiful child, and fourteen months after Jim was born our second son came along. Tom was a beautiful, healthy boy, too, but I appreciated him even less than our first baby. "Good" mothers do not resent their children so, naturally, I repressed that feeling. In many ways I was still like a child in need of love and reassurance myself. Since I did not have the love I needed, I felt very inadequate. Because of my feelings of inadequacy, I tried to compensate by doing things like keeping my house perfect and my children clean at all times. These things got to be more than I could handle so that by the time I returned to my doctor for a checkup, he suggested I see a psychiatrist.

The psychiatrist sent me home with a Minnesota Multi-Phasic Personality Inventory test to fill out and a prescription for drugs. Within a few months, I was hospitalized. Until this time I had been rather religious but there in the hospital, God and prayer did not cross my mind. I was fed pills four times a day. When I did not respond, I was given shock treatments along with the pills which left me even more confused. After a few weeks I was sent home with several kinds of pills and did not know one kind from the other. My depression continued, so once a week I was driven to the hospital for another shock treatment. I don't recall exactly how long this went on, but I don't think it was more than a couple of months. The shock treatments made me temporarily forget what had happened in the past and made it difficult to function in the present. They did not cure me as I had hoped they would.

Shock treatments are degrading to human dignity. I believe it is time for doctors to find some alternatives. Shock treatments do not heal pain; they only put it off. If psychiatric units were patterned after chemical dependency units, they would have a much higher rate of recovery. In recent years, I've observed that the people who came out of treatment for chemical dependency were off all mood-altering chemicals and functioned quite well. They had been helped to deal with reality during their hospitalization. On the other hand, people who came out of the psychiatric units were put on drugs and functioned poorly. The answer I have seen from my own personal experience and the experiences of many friends is that healing comes from the support of other people who have experienced similar pain. Healing, then, comes from support and love, not from pills and shock treatments. My hope is that more professionals will realize this fact. Lest I sound self-righteous, I want to say I also realize there are people who refuse to face reality. Those people are not the ones I am referring to. Let's find out first if that is really the case before we fill them with drugs and shock treatments. Let those alternatives be the last resort instead of the first.

Through the next couple of years I existed with pills and counseling, and then one early spring a series of tornadoes partially destroyed our home while my husband, I and our children huddled in terror under our basement steps.

Everyone involved in those tornadoes suffered deep emotional trauma. But, in my craziness, I thought God was telling me to shape up and quit taking my frustrations out on my family, and so I promised God I would try harder to control myself.

Can you see the sick ego in my believing that God sent those terrible tornadoes to give me a message? Needless to say, I ended up back in the hospital. This time I felt embarrassed about being in the hospital, so I did not want anyone else to know. After all, my brother and sister-in-law had lost everything in the tornado, and they were coping. Why couldn't I? When I unexpectedly received flowers from a group of neighbors, I was surprised and felt the flowers meant they still accepted me. I felt grateful. In the hospital this time I pleaded with the doctor to give me anything but shock treatments, and he honored my request. But he put me on heavy doses of several kinds of sedation. After three weeks in the hospital I was released, and my doctor cut the dosage of pills I was taking in half. When I got home, I started to go through such panic I was sure I was going crazy. I did not realize it at the time, but what I was experiencing was withdrawal from the pills. It was worse than hell — I was so desperate, so alone, and so afraid of death.

I can remember telling my husband in those days before E.A. that hell could not be any worse than the way I was feeling. The concept I had of hell at the time was fire and brimstone, burning and being hot, and I hated the heat. After a couple of years in E.A., I discovered that hell was not what I formerly believed. Hell is living in our own little world, cut off from others, feeling totally alone. I thought, "My God, I am living in hell here on earth." Now I believe heaven or hell are attitudes and begin in the reality of today. How we choose to deal with life today will determine where we want to be.

While I was in the throes of mental illness, two close relatives died. I noticed that others had compassion for physical illness and death, but little understanding or compassion for emotional illness. Often I had wished I had something wrong that a doctor could remove with a scalpel. Two years later I was hospitalized again with severe headaches. I thought, "This time it's physical." It wasn't. I had an anxiety attack in the hospital and ended up back on the psychiatric floor. As much as I didn't want to go back there, I was starting to feel at home on that unit.

Through E.A., I came to see that I felt safe being drugged, having no responsibility, and being taken care of. Many people in E.A. have shared this same realization in meetings. This is common, not an exception. It is great to know that we are not alone in our feelings, reactions and craziness.

I was confronted for the first time in my life with the fact that it was my choice to get well or to stay sick, to look at myself and see the pride, the self-pity, and resentments that were causing my suffering. I needed to stop using my feelings of being unique which separated me from others and perpetuated my illness.

In E.A. I was also told to stop asking why I was the way I was and start asking what I can do about it today. To ask *why* would keep me sick, to ask *what* would open the door to recovery. I was told to stop dwelling on my symptoms. They would disappear as I felt better about myself. It was time to stop looking at what others were doing and look at what I was doing. I needed to start being honest with myself. I saw how blame had to be eliminated from my vocabulary, because blaming others or myself would only keep me sick. Finally, I had to see that others had done the best they could, and that I had done the best I could. There was no way I could go back and change anything. What I needed to do was look at my past, understand it, and accept it. Then I could develop some compassion for the person I was. It was my responsibility — my response to my ability.

When I first read the words *searching* and *fearless* in Step Four, I thought taking my inventory meant I would have no fear and it would be painless. It wasn't long before I realized it meant I may be scared, but I must go ahead in openness. Hearing Carl Becherer, a hospital chaplain, at an E.A. open meeting say that pain is a part of the healing of every illness, helped me see that after all, pain is not all negative. Facing it brings about healing. He also said, "We have a tendency to be so self-critical, so unaccepting of our humanity, we need to continually reject self-rejection."

When I first saw the word *moral*, I immediately associated it with sex and stealing. It is so much more than that. Morality includes our values, our way of reacting to life, what we believe, and how we have lived in all areas — family, friends, worship, and job. I began to see that many of the values I had were unrealistic — not really values but defects of character I had picked up to try to keep from getting hurt. It looked like an overwhelming job ahead of me, but I was reassured that I was not alone. Most important, I was told, "Take it one day at a time."

CHAPTER FIVE

Trusting: it's risky, it's scary, but what's the alternative?

Nothing was harder for me than dialing the phone to make an appointment for my first Fifth Step. My old programming was powerful, "You are going to be rejected, criticized, condemned, judged and questioned." Others who had been through this process reassured me it would not be this way. The person hearing my Fifth Step, if he understood the program, would be accepting and non-judgmental and maybe even offer insight and guidance.

It was risky and scary, but what was the alternative? I knew by this time if I did not share the experiences that had surfaced from my past, I would probably have another breakdown. With that thought in mind, the phone call was easier to make. I knew I had to start to trust, because it was the only way.

I know today that what I really needed was to go to a clergyman because of all my religious hangups. Instead, I called my psychiatrist and asked him if I could talk to him. I was about four months into the program when I sat with him for half an hour. I thought he learned more about me in that short period of time than he did in all the years I had gone to him. He was accepting of what I had to say and encouraged me to stick with the program and keep him posted with my progress. Although this was not a thorough Fifth Step, it was a start.

After listening to others share their experiences with a Fifth Step, I feel it is crucial to pick first Fifth Step counselors very carefully.

My next Fifth Step was about eight months later with a clergyman who understood the program. For the first time, I shared my pain, fear, guilt and resentment from the past. I cried and cried as these experiences tumbled out. I was reassured by him that I was not unique, and that experiences similar to mine happened to many others.

My next Fifth Step came only a few months later. This time, the clergyman helped me to see I was not sick just because I was still experiencing negative emotions. "You're sick when you *don't* feel, not when you feel," he said. For the first time I realized that ambivalent emotions about many experiences were a sign of being human.

The Twelve Step program of Emotions Anonymous was in its infancy when I got into it. People were not really admitting to the return of negative feelings. They were trying to be positive so others would not become discouraged. For instance, someone would say, "I used to get angry, now I don't get angry any more," or "I used to be afraid of being rejected, but I no longer fear rejection." The reality is that no one changes that quickly and, in any given instance, old ways of feeling and reacting do come back. The difference now is that we can recognize what is going on and make new choices. There has been a great deal of growth in the fellowship and in individuals as well. Honesty has grown as we all have grown.

I made a couple of Fifth Steps with Carl Becherer, a hospital chaplain I had heard speak at an E.A. open meeting. Carl, a quiet man who listened to A.A. Fifth Steps, has much insight into people in the program. He pointed out my rationalization, my perfectionism, and my idealism. When I told him how I was trying to be aware of what was going on with me so I would not end up in the hospital again, he compared my behavior to that of an alcoholic. He pointed out to me that I used stewing, debating, worrying, analyzing, judging, rejecting, suppressing, justifying, and minimizing to get back into emotional turmoil just as an alcoholic might do to get back to drinking. In fact, with this kind of thinking, if I were an alcoholic, I would probably have started drinking again. I had thought my reason for watching every thought and action of mine was so I would not get sick again. In reality, I was doing these things so I could keep in control. Control would keep me sick. By being honest and open with where I was at, my blind areas would be pointed out to me, he said.

After Carl pointed out my perfectionism, I asked him, "How can I get rid of it?" He replied, "The more you suffer from your perfectionism, the more you will be willing to let it go." My reaction was, "Thanks a lot!" But as I have grown, what Carl had said has come to pass. My pain did help me to let go of much of my perfectionism, and I continued to learn to accept more of my humanity each day.

Another thing Carl pointed out to me was that my continual reading was an effort to find some particular phrase or paragraph that would help me feel I was acceptable. I learned a lot from my reading, and I am glad I did not give it up. As I continued to read, I remembered what Carl had said, "You will not find the answer to self-acceptance on the next page; you are an acceptable being as you are." The last couple of years, I have not felt the need to read like I used to. Maybe what Carl had told me was true. I do think I have grown to be more self-accepting. It is possible my saturation point was finally reached.

One night when Phil Hansen was talking, he referred to a priest friend of his who works with alcoholics, by saying, "He is such a good Christian, you don't notice he's a Catholic." My ears perked up when I heard this. He sounded like someone I would like to meet. Father Arnie Luger had a busy schedule of listening to Fifth Steps either in his office or at several treatment centers in the city. When I was in need of taking another Fifth Step, I called him. He seemed kind and friendly over the phone, and we set up an appointment.

Father Luger is a kind and loving man who deeply believes in the Twelve Step program. When I first met him, I was still suffering from scrupulosity (thinking I should feel guilty about parts of my humanity). This was the hardest trait for me to break. He felt I just needed to be reassured of a loving, forgiving God. He was right. Looking back, I can see the old programming had so much power over me. I would work through scrupulosity in one area, and then it would sneak up in another. Each time I faced it, however, it had less power over me.

When I became impatient with my own growth, all I needed to do was remember Father Luger and his sharing the fact that he, too, had not arrived, that he was still maturing. He was in his late sixties when I met him, and if he still needed to work on his life, who did I think I was that I should be further along than he was?

After knowing Father Luger for several years and feeling his gentle acceptance and encouragement, I began to believe even more in my worth and potential as a child of God. Through knowing Father Luger, I have become more and more in touch with the feeling of a loving God. He supported me through many experiences. Once, when I was feeling frustrated because I did not have the feeling of a conscious contact with God, he helped me see that it was unrealistic to expect a constant feeling of closeness to my Higher Power. This closeness would come and go, and I would know it in my head — not by a feeling.

I had a hard time dealing with my mother, and he helped me a lot in this relationship. Because I did not see her more often, I felt guilty. But, because she was so unhappy and negative, it was painful for me to be around her. Visiting with her stirred up all the old feelings and attitudes I was trying to let go. He helped me see that my first responsibility is to myself and my own emotional health, then to my spouse, and then to my children. My responsibility for my mother was to see that she was physically taken care of. And she was.

Father Luger was there for me, as were many of my E.A. friends, when my mother died, and when my mother- and father-in-law died. In these cases, I dealt with the grief process instead of running away from it as I had done with other deaths. I lost much of my fear of dying.

Father Luger was there to lend support when I was concerned with our son Jim's chemical use. It was a painful experience to see someone I loved hurting himself. When I blamed myself for Jim's problems, Father Luger helped me to see I had done the best I could, and that Jim was making his own choices. I had to accept that I had done the best I could.

Jim went into treatment and that helped him grow up a great deal, but, much to my disappointment, he did not stick with the program right away. Today, as a young adult, Jim is free to make his own decisions and take the consequences for them. I believe he has the ability to make the decisions that are right for him.

Father Luger was there again when I had concern for my son, Tom, and the direction his life was taking. I saw that I needed to help Tom in any way I could, but here again, feeling guilt for my past was useless. Father Luger thought the most important years for a child were the teen years and not so much the younger years as the psychology books claim. If that is the case, I can give myself a pat on the back because in these past few years I have put much time and effort into establishing an open and loving relationship with both my boys. I have been available to them when they needed me and have given them the feeling of being loved and accepted for who they are. In their times of being open, they have acknowledged that they know they are loved.

I used to get wiped out over almost everything before E.A. Father Luger helped me see my hanging on through these crises and taking what action I could was a real sign of growth and maturity. Each time we sat down he said, "We keep maturing until the day we die. We never fully mature. A good sign of maturity is being able to see our assets and accept them." Dwelling on the negative is such a copout. As long as I dwelled on the negative aspects of my personality, I did not have to take responsibility for my potential. My negativity has been tough to crack, but it is gradually losing some of its control.

Father Luger helped me see how important it is to work on being equal with others instead of playing the inferior and superior game. I need to remember that I am one among many, and that we each have something to offer.

He helped me see how, through the past years, I have been moving away from my need for approval from specific people and how I have been gaining some distance in relationships where I felt more dependency. He saw me develop an adult conscience — not doing things out of fear, but because I know I am loved. He watched me move away from rejecting myself, to seeing my faults and mistakes, and realizing they will always be there. They are part of my humanity.

I made a Fifth Step with Father Luger just a couple of weeks ago in the midst of some heavy family turmoil. I talked about some of my negative qualities and for the first time I did not cry because they were there. I even surprised myself by my concentration on the improvement and change in my life, and I did not worry about sounding proud. I felt a lot of gratitude. His response was so beautiful. He told me of the tremendous growth he had seen since I first sat down with him. He remembered how

I had cried each time, because I was unable to accept my human imperfections. He encouraged me to write this book because I had "a lot to offer." He felt my growth had come because of my relationship with my Higher Power. I know this is true. "Remember, nothing can happen that is so bad God cannot make good come out of it," he said. I believed that, too. In spite of all the pain our family had been through, I had not doubted God's care or love.

Father Luger is in his seventies today. I've thought about how sad I will feel when he is gone. It will be a great personal loss. Looking back, I can see how I've needed each person's particular personality and sensitivity at the time they were there. Each relationship that God put in my life helped me become more dependent on my Higher Power. I know there will always be someone to help me with any need I will ever have for I have made many wonderful friends in E.A. and A.A. who are as near as the telephone.

My early Fifth Step experiences gave me a tremendous release, because I was clearing out the pain from the past. The subsequent Fifth Steps were not as exhilarating, because I was dealing with problems in the present. Each Fifth Step gave me what I needed at the time. It was well worth putting my fear and pride aside and going ahead with each Fifth Step. Reaching out to the clergy for my needs helped me gain more confidence and trust in myself and helped me let go of my rigidity. I no longer feel the overwhelming need to be reassured. If some emergency comes up when I feel I need someone to talk to like Father Luger, I can pick up the phone and call. Now, as I feel the need, I take the Fourth and Fifth Steps once or twice a year. I do not believe I would have the freedom I have today if I hadn't reached out to get my need for encouragement and reassurance met. I am grateful for my past pain, because I believe that if I had not hurt so much, my pride and my fear might have won out. The people who listened to me and gave me so much of themselves will always have a special place in my heart.

CHAPTER SIX

Only God is perfect

I remember thinking, "I am ready to have all my symptoms and pain removed." It took some time before I understood the implications of this and before I realized the commitment this would involve. Through my Fourth and Fifth Steps and my weekly meetings, I continued learning about myself.

One of the first defects I recognized was my need to be perfect. Most of my other defenses stemmed from my perfectionism. Before Emotions Anonymous, when people would tell me I was a perfectionist, I took it as a compliment. In E.A., I learned my perfectionism was a defense to avoid criticism. I could not be criticized if I were perfect, could I? As a result of trying to be perfect, I got into the pattern of self-criticism. I hadn't avoided criticism after all; in fact, I criticized myself more than others ever did because I could never measure up to my own standards. I did not realize human beings were not meant to be perfect — only God is perfect.

I recall hearing the expression, "Be perfect as your Heavenly Father is perfect." I took this to mean I should be just like God. What it means to me today is that I should be as perfect as a human being is capable of being. To me this means to develop my potential. Who can relate to someone who is setting himself above another? Trying to be perfect is lonely.

I remember Jess Lair saying, "If we humans were to make up a recipe for our personality, we would include patience, kindness, love, tolerance, generosity, understanding, etc." These are all virtues that relate to God, leaving no room for our human characteristics. We do not include characteristics that help us relate to people and make us realize our need for a Higher Power.

As a child, my perfectionism revolved around trying to be

"good." When I wasn't able to be as good as I thought I should be, I then became obsessed with my appearance as a teenager. After I married, I tried to keep our home perfect. I realize now how shallow it was to have my worth as a person measured by how I looked and how I kept my house. Dressing nice and having a clean house are values for me to retain, but not to the point where they will ever control my life again. Although I do like to look nice, I no longer worry about my appearance. I no longer compulsively clean house, either. This new behavior feels really good. Today, when someone unexpectedly stops in and my home looks lived in, I am comfortable. I am grateful my feelings of worth come more from being who I am rather than from trying to prove myself. My rigid behavior came from my perfectionism. I felt that everything should fall under one of two categories — right or wrong.

Although rigidity seemed safe and secure, this defense was destructive because it kept me from becoming a mature and responsible adult. Now I realize I was being rigid in an attempt to stay close to God, but actually there was a fear in my rigidity which kept me further away from God. Rigidity also caused feelings of self-righteousness and superiority which kept me separate from other people. Defining right and wrong is not always so simple. I have come to see that what is wrong in one instance might be right in another, and what is right in one instance might be wrong in another. There are many times when the choice in a situation is neither right nor wrong. Often there are many alternatives, none of which is wrong, just a matter of preference.

Idealism also comes from perfectionism. Setting unattainable goals for myself was a pattern I developed at an early age. At the time most of these ideals seemed to make me feel safe and free from self-rejection. After growing up and getting into the outside world, these ideals were impossible to live up to, so my world came crashing in on me. Not wanting to accept my humanity made me no less human and did not make it go away. Now I know that accepting myself and what I see around me is a daily process toward maturity and peace of mind.

My compulsive behavior also caused me to feel anxiety and an urgency to get everything done *now*. What helped me to stop this

was to say, "Easy Does It" and "First Things First." This would
slow me down so I could think about what was most important.
If I see some compulsive behavior in myself today, I stop and
look at what I am feeling anxious about. Is it something I can take
some action on? If I can, I get with it because I no longer feel at
home with turmoil. It is easy to take action when I am not trying
to be perfect. Since I no longer am trying to be perfect, I don't feel
failure if my actions don't always resolve a problem. At least I
know I have done my best for the present so I can fall asleep at
night without feeling guilty.

Scrupulosity caused me to have an exaggerated feeling of guilt
for not living up to an unrealistic expectation of myself. I used to
run away from my humanity. It was a sign of other conflicts that I
wanted to ignore, because I felt unable to change them. If I was
busy worrying about something trivial, it kept me from dealing
with the real problem. Scrupulosity was another way of
expressing anxiety. If I center back on trivia again, I stop and ask
myself, "What is the *real* problem right now?"

My obsessive thinking was somewhat like my compulsiveness
and my scrupulosity in the sense that it was an outlet for my
anxiety. My obsessive thoughts kept me from dealing with reality
for days. I was afraid to see my real self, but the more I ran from
myself, the more control my obsessive thinking had over me. My
obsessions kept me from facing my humanity. My obsessive
thinking was yet another way to cover up areas of conflict in my
life. It was not a sign that I was going crazy. Like my
compulsiveness and scrupulosity, obsessions kept me centered
on some trivia which, in turn, kept me from dealing with any real
feelings of guilt, or embarrassment, or anger, or such, that I really
needed to deal with.

After being in E.A. a while, I discovered my depressions were
frozen rage. Depression kept the lid on my self-pity, resentments,
fear, anger, my enormous guilt, and my sadness. Depression was
my silent attempt to change reality. In my depression, I was "on
strike" against life, because life had not seemed fair to me. In
withdrawing, I was saying, "See how badly I already hurt? Please
don't hurt me any more." In my deepest depression, I became
non-functional so those around me needed to step in to care for
me. My depression became a way of learned helplessness.

Today, when I feel myself becoming depressed, I am aware

that I am angry with some reality of life or with someone's behavior, neither of which I can control or change. I also see a part of me that would like to use that depression again to manipulate another to change. Seeing my honest feelings and realizing what I want to do puts me in touch with my past. Remembering my past and the pain depression caused me, I think, "In no way am I going to let outside circumstances or another person's behavior make me that sick again. I have come too far and appreciate my peace of mind too much." Then I can usually let go of my wanting to be depressed.

At other times I can become depressed because I feel I am procrastinating. When I am afraid of taking action or making a decision, I pray for guidance and get moving. A wrong decision is better than no decision if the alternative is depression.

Whether I call it anxiety, panic, acute anxiety, agoraphobia, or incapacitating fear, it all means the same to me. When I became anxious, it ranged from loss of control to impending disaster, such as death. In my panic, I felt as though I needed to run, yet, at the same time, I was not able to take another breath. I believed that my increasing panic was a sign I was closer to going crazy. In E.A., I came to see that the anxiety I was experiencing had nothing to do with my real problem. Trying to figure out why I was so anxious in a particular situation only increased my anxiety.

My feeling of anxiety came from wanting to run away from or to control myself, my feelings, or some reality of life. Beneath my anxiety I often found a fear of being hurt or a fear of losing something. In addition to the same feelings I experienced during depressions, in anxiety there was a stronger emphasis on fear, anger, and guilt.

The more I have been able to express all of my feelings to friends in E.A. and to accept myself as I am, no matter what, the less problem I have with anxiety. I need to reach out to people daily and not store up my feelings. In doing so, I have not had an anxiety attack for years. For that I am extremely grateful. I still have my anxious moments when some problem or tragedy occurs that I cannot control, but as long as I can talk about what I am feeling, accept reality, and accept where I am at, panic does not return.

Like depression, anxiety can also come if there is a decision I refuse to make because I fear the outcome. Living with that constant state of turmoil is worse than my fear of the outcome. Trusting in God's love, care, and guidance, and realizing He wants better for me than I want for myself helps me to move forward at that time.

My thoughts of wanting to die really frightened me, because I was afraid I might lose control, take my life, and then be condemned to hell forever. All of these feelings that were part of my depression and anxiety (plus feelings of hopelessness and helplessness) caused me to despair. When despair took over, suicidal thoughts were sure to follow. From the E.A. program I learned my suicidal thoughts did not mean I really wanted to die, but that I wanted to die from the way of life that was slowly killing me. Facing my feelings, especially my anger at life for being unfair, and letting go of much of my idealism caused my suicidal thoughts to leave.

Being able to sleep only a couple of hours each night for weeks at a time increased my panic. My sleepless nights became a time of terror because my thoughts were filled with worry, guilt, failure, fear, despair, and often an anxiety attack. I later learned insomnia was a problem that would leave when I felt better about myself. Here again, facing my true feelings was the key. I heard others talking about their attitude concerning sleep, saying that even if they spent some sleepless nights, it didn't hurt them. They would stop telling themselves they needed to sleep. They replaced their negative thoughts with "It doesn't matter how much sleep I get, just relaxing can give me the rest I need." These people had stopped letting worry and fearful thoughts consume them by repeating slogans like "Let Go and Let God" or "This Too Shall Pass."

Because I was experiencing insomnia when I came to E.A., I tried these new ideas, and they started to work, but it took constant discipline. I also learned to tell myself that nighttime is a time for trusting God. He gave me these hours to be able to let go and to realize that His care of me and the entire universe goes on and on. When I developed more trust in a loving Higher Power and was able to forgive myself and others, my insomnia eventually left.

Today when I am faced with a serious problem, I sometimes

find myself waking up after only a few hours of sleep. When I do, I say the Serenity Prayer, "Let Go and Let God," and "Be still and know that God is with you." If after an hour I am still awake, I get up and read my meditation books, write for awhile, and ask for guidance. The wisdom to know the best decision usually does not come quickly, but it does eventually come by my being open. I know that a decision I make out of love, without resentment, anger, or self-pity, will give me the peace of mind I desire. After filling my thoughts with something positive for awhile, I can usually go back to sleep.

I've also found a new attitude about worry. I used to worry about many things. I thought worry was a virtue, that it meant I really cared about someone. Actually, worry is useless and very exhausting. Worry keeps me from taking responsible action in the present. Now I see that to worry is to play God. It is trying to handle what only a Higher Power can handle. Worry is fearing something in the future. How can I possibly project what will happen? Usually the things I worried about never happened anyway. I heard once, "Worry is the punishment we get for not trusting God." Another time I heard, "If you are going to pray, why worry; and if you are going to worry, why pray?"

I came to the program wanting to be well instantly. It had taken me years to get sick, and it would take time to get well, too. But the old programming was powerful, and I needed to be patient when it surfaced again. To recognize my old attitudes and be grateful that I could see them now would help me to make new choices. When I was very new in the program and someone would say to me, "Just be patient," I felt like screaming. I wanted what I wanted immediately. I remember someone kiddingly saying, "God grant me patience — and do it right now."

I had been aware of my impatience with my children and felt guilty about it. I had not been aware of how impatient I had been with myself. Why shouldn't I give myself the same regard that I give to another person? I prayed for patience, yet it seemed like new things would come into my life that could not be resolved overnight. What did I gain through this? More patience! I was told I was gaining patience simply because I was aware of my lack of it.

Because of my own fear, many of the things I wanted to

happen so badly could not happen. One of the common denominators of people coming to E.A. is their inability to handle the good. For that reason the good has to come slowly. I believe patience is tied to trusting in a loving Higher Power. If I can really believe that He gives me what I need (although it may not necessarily be what I think I want), it is easier to wait. God does things at just the right time and in ways I can't comprehend. As soon as He sees I can handle the good I want, He gives it to me.

I have been a person who didn't like having things unresolved. It gave me a good reason to stew. Today I am living with a couple of unresolved situations, and the only way I can keep my sanity is to pray for the patience to wait. Learning that patience is developed by dealing with stressful situations helps me see I have become more patient. But my impatience can come back in any given situation, and when it does, I need to take it to my Higher Power and ask for His help. I saw a poster at a neighbor's house that said, "Patience is the doorway to joy." To me, joy means the ability to live with some peace of mind, even with unresolved problems. Realizing how important patience is to my peace of mind, I thought it worth the effort to develop.

I had not realized how much I used pleasing as a tool to gain acceptance. Unknowingly, I did many things to gain the love I so desperately needed. I tried to be the way I thought others wanted me to be, or I tried to be like other people who seemed to be happy and well-liked. I wanted everyone's approval and since that is impossible, I had feelings of frustration and low self-worth. The reality is that there are a few people who will really like me the way I am and a few who won't. But the majority of the people fall into the category of indifference. In trying to please everyone, there is no guarantee of anyone being satisfied, but if I please myself, at least one person is happy.

As a pleaser, I worried what others were thinking of me. In first grade, I didn't know anyone and didn't want to. In high school, I projected that others would not want to talk to me so I would walk down the hall pretending no one else was there. At the same time I was thinking, "Boy, are they snobs; they won't even say hello." Thinking critically of others helped me to keep others at a distance.

As an adult I still felt uncomfortable around others so I

projected that they did not want to be around me. Here again, it was my own fear of self. My worst projections came when I was really sick. I felt others were watching me, talking about me, and putting me down because of my illness. Even after being in E.A., I still used projection. Once I had shared something with someone, and the next time I talked to him I felt he was not accepting me. Seeing through what I was doing, he threw the responsibility back at me saying, "What does it matter what I think?" When he turned the responsibility back to me, I realized I was the one who wasn't accepting what I had said. He had accepted me just fine.

I will never forget someone in E.A. saying to me, "What makes you think you are so important that other people are watching you and talking about you?" It was then I saw the egotism in my projecting. I was relieved to realize that other people were usually more involved with themselves and their own problems and not really that concerned about me. I could begin to look at people and not fear that they were watching me or talking about me. This insight gave me more freedom to be myself.

Projection became a copout. If I saw the other person as being responsible for how I was feeling about myself, there was no action I could take to help myself. Projection is so sneaky and subtle that it actually seems like the feeling is coming from the other person. If I start thinking someone is feeling a particular way about me, I ask myself if it is something the other person feels or if it is really my own feeling about myself? From my projection came my defenses of blaming. If other people would just act differently and treat me differently, I would feel okay about myself. Then came the self-pity because others did not respond the way I thought they should. After all, "others" were responsible for the way I felt and behaved.

In E.A., I began to see the power I had given others over my life. I began to realize it was not the responsibility of others to make me feel anything; it was mine. At first it was scary to realize I was in charge of my life. Maybe I might not have the stamina to make it. On the other hand, I was relieved to see that others were not responsible for my happiness. If they were, I would have to sit and wait for them to fix me up. Because I was responsible, I could start today to change my outlook on life.

As far back as I can remember I felt insecure. Now I see my insecurity came because I was counting on myself to handle my life. I did not want to count on others, and I did not trust God. Sometimes when I hear someone new to E.A. say, "I'm insecure," I hear my old self in them. I remember wearing my insecurity badge which said, "Treat me gentle, I am fragile." I see now it was a way I used to try to manipulate others to take care of me. The way I got rid of some insecurity was by starting to trust in someone outside myself. Today I feel much more secure, and I know it comes from the love I have received from others, which in turn, has helped me realize God's love and care.

Shyness was a characteristic of mine since early childhood. Now I see shyness as a defense rather than a reality. Behind my shyness was a fear of people and a fear of myself. By my being shy the responsibility of a relationship rested on the other person. Seeing my shyness as self-centeredness helped me to want to let it go.

In procrastination I found a great deal of anger and self-pity. Either someone was expecting more from me than I was able to give or wanted to give, or I was promising more than I could deliver. So then a part of me rebelled. Attitude has so much to do with procrastination. If I find myself letting things pile up, it helps me to first do the thing I hate the most. From doing the job I most dislike, energy starts to flow again and the rest of the tasks become easier. Oftentimes, in procrastinating, I am trying to punish another person who may have some expectations of me. I end up hurting myself most because a lot of energy is used up in procrastinating that could go into something productive and creative that would make me feel good about myself.

After being in E.A. a few months, I became really intolerant of others who were screwed up but were not getting help. It did not seem fair that they could get away with their negativity; that it did not cause them to break down. Recognizing my intolerance, I felt guilty, but as I shared it, I learned it was a process that others had also gone through. Focusing on my intolerance and criticism of others kept me from looking at myself and the areas of my life I needed to work on. Later, I discovered that the things I criticized in others were what I disliked most in myself. Today, instead of feeling critical and intolerant of others, I have developed some compassion for them. This is because I have come to have some understanding of myself. I am grateful that I did break down, that I could no longer stand the kind of life I was living. I feel fortunate to have found a way out of my hell. I can only hope others who are hurting will come to see they do not have to live that way.

Although I thought I was quite self-sufficient, I was a dependent person trying to act independent. Because I did not want to experience the pain of being let down or the pain of losing someone I cared about again, I did not want to need anyone.

Until I became so depressed that I lost the ability to function, I had never been aware of my dependency. When I expected my husband to support me in all areas and he couldn't, I resented him. I really thought he should be able to meet all of my needs and make me happy. After all, isn't that what marriage is all about? When I felt my husband failed me, I became dependent on a sister who lived nearby. Because no one was able to make me feel good enough about myself, I became dependent on pills for my happiness.

One of the sayings in our program is, "Never put a person on a pedestal because all humans have feet of clay." What I was really saying to the person I put on the pedestal was, "You can do it because you have all the answers. Poor me, I am so helpless." It is neither a compliment nor love to expect from others what we should be doing for ourselves. When I expect too much from people, I turn them off. Then I can feel rejected, and it gives me the excuse to say to myself, "I'm hopeless; I'm just a burden; life is just too hard." Again, I would have an excuse to copout.

Accepting that I am a dependent person while looking for healthy ways to meet that dependency is a challenge I have been able to meet to a large degree through the E.A. program. There is a healthy dependence that I call inter-dependence. God made us to need others to survive. We cannot meet our needs for love by ourselves, but we are responsible for having our needs met. I discovered that there were many people in my life who could give me what I needed. All I had to do was be honest, open, and willing to receive from them. If I could not accept the gift of love from other people, how could I ever be able to accept the greatest gift of all, God's love? I came to see I could not buy love, and I do not have to earn love. Love is a free gift. The fact that we exist means we are entitled to receive it.

For some time after I came into the program I still thought some of my problems were unique, like my obsession to count everything in my house. As long as we hang on to the idea that any of our quirks are that different or unique, it keeps us locked into the problem, and we are unable to be open to the help available in the program. While I was preoccupied with my compulsiveness, my obsessions, my scrupulosity, depression, anxiety, and my suicidal thoughts, I found it impossible to relate to others. Being afraid of dealing with people, my illness became a substitute for relationships.

A few years ago I attended a weekend workshop dealing with attitudes. One attitude that continued to cause me trouble was the fear I had of getting close to my husband and then being separated from him by death, like my father. Because I wanted to see if I could break through that fear, the person leading the workshop told me to walk around to each person and say, "I can love you, and you won't die." Self-consciously I repeated this to about five people, and suddenly I said to the next person, "I can love you, and I won't die." It hit me like a ton of bricks! It wasn't that I was still afraid of getting close for fear of losing Jim. Unconsciously, I was afraid I would still have to die (give up my identity) to gain his love. I was damned if I would ever give up my identity again for anyone's acceptance. What I have discovered since that awareness is that I do not have to give up my identity to gain someone's love. People who really love me do not want me to be a carbon copy of them. They want me to be free to develop my own potential as that is the way I can bring something back into the relationship.

Many times I felt guilty about certain behaviors of mine, such as picking a fight with Jim or screaming at the boys when I was really upset about other things. The way I have found to break this habit is to deal with my feelings in the present, take responsibility for them, and not let them build up. When I can say *I* feel sad, hurt, angry, or lonely instead of *you make me* feel sad, hurt, angry, or lonely, then the other person can listen without getting defensive. What other people do can cause me to feel sad, hurt, angry or lonely. What I *do* with that feeling is what I am responsible for.

Becoming entirely ready for all our defects to be removed will be a lifetime process. We need to be patient and remind ourselves to look for progress, not perfection. When we are hanging on to a defect, not wanting to let it go, we need to remember to pray for the willingness to let it go. Then we need to replace the defect with some positive asset.

I have never been able to eliminate a defect by an act of will power. By acknowledging the defect's presence and turning it over to my Higher Power, it can be removed, if He sees fit. If it isn't removed, maybe it's because I need to do more work on the positive. Our Higher Power will not remove a defect until we have found an asset to take its place. If something I think of as a defect is not removed, it may be just a part of my personality that I will have to accept. In the past, many characteristics that I thought were virtues turned out to be defects.

There were times in the early years when I would have liked to have done without all this "wonderful insight." It seemed to make my life more complicated. But today I see that was another defense against seeing my humanity. Facing myself honestly and seeing my defenses was scary and painful, because I had run from myself for so many years. If I remember that my defects are not virtues but defenses I put up to protect myself, I can see they do me more harm than good. Then it is easier for me to let go. More importantly, my defects create my symptoms, and my symptoms are a barrier that keeps me from receiving the love I need to make my existence meaningful.

CHAPTER SEVEN

Man's need — God's opportunity

"Not until man has failed can he learn the true meaning of humility."* I was wondering how I was going to start this chapter, and this morning in one of my meditation books these words leaped from the pages.

It wasn't until I thought I had no resources left that God was able to step in to help me. He pulled me away from my despair, hopelessness, self-centeredness, and manipulating ways. Trying for years to change had accomplished nothing. Finally, I could see all my attempts for help had been blocked by pride and fear. That's when God started to change me into a more loving and caring person. How could I take any credit?

Humility was a word I misunderstood until I came to Emotions Anonymous. I used to think humility meant you put yourself below others, you did not feel as though you had anything to offer, you suffered, you denied yourself, you acted holy, you prayed, and you observed all the rules. Humility, to me, meant I should feel inferior.

Now I see humility in a totally new light. Humility accepts its strengths as well as its weaknesses. Humility feels neither inferior nor superior. It recognizes our need for a Higher Power in our life and puts us in proper perspective to that Power. Humility sees its need to let go of self-will, and it also recognizes that we each have something special to offer as a child of God.

Today, I see pride in a new way also. I think there is a healthy pride that could have the same definition as humility — accepting our strengths as well as our weaknesses. But, as I talk about pride in this book, I do not refer to it in a positive way.

Twenty-four Hours a Day, Hazelden Educational Materials, Box 176, Center City, MN. 55012.

I have learned about false pride. False pride is destructive. It is a pretense and a lie. False pride places expectations on ourselves and others to try to be something we are not. With it I can say I am great, I am better than others, I am terrible, or I am worse than others, none of which is true.

False pride is seen in the game of inferior/superior. I remember feeling inferior and looking at the person who acted superior. I thought I was a better person, because I felt inferior. I was feeling superior about feeling inferior. I used to think I had to be better than others to be equal with them. I used to believe the person who acted so arrogant and superior really felt he was, but I have come to see that that person felt just as inadequate and insecure about himself as I did.

Walther Lechler, a German psychiatrist I met through the program who had a great sense of humor, said, "If you feel inferior, it is because you are." By this he meant we need to learn and to grow in the area where we feel inferior, and then we will stop feeling that way. If we are feeling inferior in every area, we should see if maybe we are using feeling inferior to escape taking some responsibility for our life. I was shocked one day to hear Jess Lair say, "The only reason a person feels inferior is that he thinks he is supposed to be superior." Did that hit me! If I did not think I was supposed to be so great, so much better than I was, I would not feel inferior. What right did I have to make the judgment that I was inferior. God had made me as I was for some purpose. To always be putting myself down was to put myself above God. Jess believes that a person who seems to put himself above another is doing so because he feels inferior himself. Neither inferiority nor superiority are healthy attitudes, because they both cause us to feel separate and different from others.

Comparing myself to others was one of my most damaging shortcomings, because it usually brought on feelings of inferiority and helplessness. Why couldn't I be like my sister, my girlfriend, or anyone? I did not want to be me. Comparing caused me to feel I didn't measure up. So why even try? "I will never be able to be the person I want to be." Comparing also caused me to feel jealous.

When I felt inferior for too long, I needed to tear someone else down by finding their faults and judging them by my own values. Then I would feel superior. But when I felt superior, I felt guilty so I would put myself down for being critical, and then I would feel inferior again. I felt more comfortable with inferiority. Too bad I did not feel guilty about feeling inferior, maybe my game would have stopped sooner.

Comparing was such a pattern in my life, it was hard to let it go, but I could see it was a copout for not developing my own identity. Today, if I compare myself to someone, I stop and say, "Hey, how come you want to run from your own capabilities? You have something to offer just being the person you are." If I want to compare as a constructive tool, it is okay to look back at my own growth, comparing where I have been and how far I have come. This creates a feeling of gratitude, which, in turn, opens me up to more good to come into my life.

My jealousy was subtle and caused me to feel competitive toward others. Either I wanted what someone else had, or I wanted to be able to do what someone else could do. When I recognized that by being jealous I was not acknowledging my own worth, I realized I could let go of jealousy by developing my own abilities. As I began to grow and could see some of my abilities, I wanted to do what I saw others were doing because I felt capable of doing it, too. Sometimes it seemed unfair that others were given the opportunity to do something I was not. Then one day I realized that no one can keep our good from us. What God really wants us to do, He will find a way for us to do. Realizing God is in charge of the good in my life and gives me the opportunities I can handle when I am ready for them, I no longer need to be threatened by someone else's talents. Instead, I can be happy for them and their chance for growth. God's gift of talent to one person never limits another person.

I need to see that my goals for each day are realistic. When I was new in the program, just making it through one day was as much as I could expect of myself. If I expected too much and did not live up to it, then I felt guilty and thought I had failed. Guilt and failure locked me into more guilt and failure.

In order to stop setting myself up with unrealistic goals in those early days, I asked myself, "What would I expect of another person today who is in my shoes?" I would pretend I was talking to that person and say, "Hang in there and take it just five minutes at a time. You are okay where you're at, and when you can start accepting that, you will have the freedom to change. Replace the negative thinking with something positive like one of the slogans. Two thoughts cannot exist at the same moment. If you fall down, pick yourself back up again and be patient with yourself. Remember, you are not failing if you are trying. Even if it seems like you have failed, it doesn't necessarily mean you have. It might just mean you need to take another direction. Reach out and talk to others who understand. Get to an extra meeting."

In striving for perfection I had always fallen short of my goal, and this diminished my self-worth. Most of my life I tried to get my self-worth by *doing* rather than by *being*. One day I might feel good over a certain accomplishment only to be down in the pits again the next day. I did not understand that self-worth could not come from just *doing*.

I never suspected my feelings of worth could come from just getting out my true feelings. Getting those feelings out in the open also causes them to change. Being who I really am gives me a feeling of self-worth. Yes, I need to do things, to set some goals and meet new challenges, but that comes in a good way only after I feel I am worthwhile just by being.

As I continue to write about pride and false pride, I will be using these two terms synonymously. I heard once that, "Pride is taking glory that belongs only to God." At my entry into E.A., I felt hopeless, helpless, and useless. When I experienced insight and new-found abilities, I felt proud, and it caused me to feel I was special. I actually recall thinking that because of all the changes that were occurring in my life, God must have something special for me to do. People who had known me when I had been helpless, withdrawn, and rigid were amazed at the changes in me. I received compliments from many people. Along with enjoying this feeling of being special, I also felt frightened. I knew enough about recovery to realize that I, like the alcoholic, had what I had only for this one day by the Grace of God. Knowing how damaging pride was, as I received compliments, I acknowledged God and the people who helped me. Then instead of pride, I felt gratitude.

I came to realize that God had done things with a big impact in my life to get my attention, to give me hope. He had done these things not because I was special, but because I was so far away from him. If I had been close, He could have tapped me with a feather; because I was so distant, He had to hit me with a hammer. At first this insight deflated my ego, but this was necessary at that time. Then I felt a deep sense of gratitude for the continued effort God had made to reach me. He really met me where I was at, and He will do the same for anybody. I realize now I needed that feeling of being special for that period of time because I tended to get discouraged so easily. Remembering God's care and my commitment to Him, I could never give up when I felt like it and go back to my old ways. There remained no doubt in my mind that this program would work and that this was where God wanted me to continue to get my help.

I'll never forget how I felt when reading in an A.A. book that dwelling on the negative is pride in reverse. Putting myself down and saying I was worse than others was not humility as I had thought, but pride. Recognizing that my constant rejection of myself was really pride, I realized I had enough pride to sink a battleship. Feeling certain that sharing my pride would bring me rejection, I was fearful and hesitant to tell anyone about my new insight. But when I felt enough pain, I was more than willing to share it, and again I received acceptance and understanding.

Many times I used the excuse of holding back from trying a new challenge because I feared becoming proud. In a quiet time by myself I had some helpful insight about pride and fear. I wondered, "If you wanted to get a job done, would you ask a fearful man or a proud man to do it?" Think about it for a moment. The fearful man would be afraid, afraid of making a mistake and being criticized so he might hesitate, procrastinate, and maybe not even finish the job. The proud man would get in there and tackle the job and maybe even have a feeling of pride. In his effort to finish the job, the proud man would end up being humble because he had used his humanity to the fullest thereby accepting his human limitations. There is more pride in the fearful man not wanting to try than in the proud man trying.

Because I feared that I would appear arrogant and superior, I had a difficult time accepting the good in myself. What finally helped me to start accepting the good in myself was watching how a friend of mine related to others. I could see that he accepted his good qualities and yet did not come across as proud. He seemed to have the capacity to accept his strengths as well as his weaknesses. Now I see that is what made him so well-loved. Seeing his example helped me realize that if I really like myself, I will not appear arrogant. When I accept my strengths and my weaknesses and am grateful, I will be kept humble.

I need to keep in mind that because I am human, anything I do, even my most unselfish act will have pride at its center. The perfect, prideless motive will never be. Recognizing this reality helps me see my need for the close guidance of my Higher Power in my life.

I remember how ambivalent I was when I first became aware of my feelings of being special and the pride I felt. People complimented me, and I would feel grateful, but I would also think, "I deserve to have what I've got. I have worked so hard for it." There were times when someone seemed to be hanging onto the negative, and I would think self-righteously, "If you would just get off your duff you could have what I have, too." Then I would remember it was not virtue that led me to the Twelve Steps, it was desperation. When you do something because you are afraid that you will die if you don't, it can hardly be called virtuous. Every time it comes to my mind I thank God for my desperation, because remembering it has continued to give me my desire to recover.

In this past year my husband and I have seen a marriage counselor, Tom Wright. Tom said to me, "Not everyone wants to get well as badly as you do. People have to have a vision." I thought about my vision and realized it started out as desperation. It was only after a couple of months in the program that I felt hope and could begin to see there was purpose for every life. Why else would we be here?

If you are at the point where you don't know if getting well is worth the discipline involved, might I suggest that you pray for the desire to want to be well? I guess that is the gift I was given — an intense desire to continue growing and getting well. I believe God will give that gift to anyone who truly wants it.

Getting well brings maturity, and that helps us to see our responsibility. Being responsible is frightening, but the positive results open us to receive love and then to be able to give it to others. Love is the most wonderful natural high; so much better than any pills I ever took. Some recent studies have shown that love is not only an emotional need, but a biological need as well. I see now that love was what I was always looking for, and I know how I need it to survive. I think to love is to experience some heaven here on earth.

Jim and I were talking with Tom about receiving compliments. He shared another idea on this topic. "Throughout our lives we look to people we admire. They may stand for principles we believe in, or they may handle themselves in a way we would like to be able to. A child learns by imitating. As adults, we continue to look up to certain people. On the other hand, people may admire us. People can improve their own self-image by admiring qualities in others. Being a successful adult in any fashion may bring admiration from others. This can be satisfying, but it can also bring on feelings of responsibility. The most positive thing to do when someone compliments us is to say, thank you, and let the person know we enjoyed the compliment. By openly admitting your enjoyment in being admired, we will build the self-esteem of the person who admires us. If they identify with our values, and we reject their admiration, they may feel discouraged or confused." Since that insight, I find it much easier to enjoy a compliment without making an ego trip out of it.

A good leader is one who stands under and supports others to grow and to take responsibility, not one who gets in and tries to force others to grow in a specific way. Leadership is supportive and encouraging, not domineering and controlling. We really have no right to get into people's affairs and make decisions for them. That would only keep them from growing and learning to stand on their own two feet. This idea of leadership does not scare me. If I am a leader, at least I do not have to feel responsible for others. With the support and encouragement I have received has come a feeling of freedom and trust in my own decision-making process.

I had heard so much about the untapped potential of human beings, but I never used to believe it. Today, I see others and myself using many abilities we weren't aware we had in the past. Where did they come from? From risking and following the guidance that only comes from a Higher Power. I had always been afraid of risking for fear of being criticized. A few years ago I heard something I need to remember, "If you are getting a kick in the rear, at least that means you are out in front." There is still a part of me that wants everyone to like me. If I go out and take a risk, everyone is not going to like me or approve of me. What I need to remember is that it is more important that I like myself and feel I'm doing what I believe is right for me.

I believe a shortcoming is a reasonable expectation that we have not lived up to. I believe it is reasonable for us to expect ourselves to be responsible for ourselves and our actions each day. It is reasonable for us to expect ourselves to grow into a more kind, loving, patient, tolerant, and understanding person; but not overnight.

It is not reasonable for us to think we will ever be entirely free of our self-centeredness, our neuroses, or our human imperfections. It is not reasonable for us to expect a complete change in our personalities. Trying to change my personality, which was what I had tried to do for years, only led me to frustration. Our basic personality is God given, and we need to accept it in order for it to become an asset in our lives. Many times in the past few years I have wished I would not feel so intensely. Because the intensity of my feelings has not diminished, I am coming to believe it is a basic part of my character. The more acceptance I have for all my feelings and my need to express them, the more contentment I find, even during troubled times.

When we are praying to have our shortcomings removed, we need to remember to be patient. It may have taken years to develop our attitudes. It might take years to change many of the really ingrained ones. There's enough time, "one day at a time," to change whatever our High Power sees fit to change. God will remove our shortcomings, but He will not remove our human limitations.

CHAPTER EIGHT

Products of our past — but not victims of the past

I believe we are the product of all our past experiences, but more important than actual experiences is our perception of them and how we choose to handle these experiences today.

I could still blame my father's death for my not wanting to get close to someone today for fear they might die. I could still blame the nuns I had in grade school with their negative approach to God for my belief in a punishing God today. I could still blame my religious training for my negative attitudes about sex and for my not being able to handle sex in my marriage today. I could still blame the relative who took advantage of me sexually for my never trusting another man. I could still blame my family background for not giving me a feeling of belonging and my continuing to feel low self-worth today.

Then I could blame myself for the way I interpreted my experiences and the hurt I caused others. I could go on and on with the blame. But where would it get me?

Blaming was something that I needed to deal with so I could start to eliminate that word from my vocabulary. As long as I blamed others or myself, I would stay sick and locked into my negative behavior. It does not matter how or why we got to where we are. What does matter is that we are willing to change today. What effort are we willing to make to get well?

Almost everyone has a history of some traumatic experiences. I have to ask myself why I chose to remember mostly the negative ones. Did feeling sorry for myself give me some satisfaction? Was I afraid of being responsible? Today I realize that I mistook people feeling sorry for me as love. I also know, too, I was afraid of responsibility because I did not want to question anything or say no for fear someone might not like me.

Step Eight says, "Made a list of people we had harmed," not of those who harmed me. There were situations where I felt harmed by others, but I had to see the part I played. If I let myself be used or hurt repeatedly, why did I continue to follow that pattern? Did being a martyr bring me some feelings of superiority or of being in control?

If I ever wanted to be happy and function as a whole person in the present or in the future, I needed to see things as they were and make peace with my past. Certainly I had a lot of reasons for my resentments and self-pity. But I began to see that hanging on to those reasons was only hurting me. True, this pain had to be dealt with in Steps Four and Five, but then I needed to let go and take responsibility for my happiness today.

I looked at the relationships that came up in my Fourth and Fifth Steps. I needed to make amends to those I felt anger and resentment toward. I also needed to make amends to those people closest to me who I had hurt by my illness.

The people I held resentment for were near the top of my list. Learning that resentment and self-pity caused so many of my painful symptoms, I was eager to let them go. A clergyman spoke at the first retreat I attended for Twelve Step members. He talked about the resentments he felt toward his parents. By coming to understand them and their background, he was able to let the resentment go. Understanding them gave him some compassion for his parents. Then he could see that they had done the best they could.

I decided I also needed to understand my family's background in order to let go of resentment, have compassion and set myself free. I knew little about my father's background except that he came from a family of four brothers and one sister. My dad was a hard-working truck farmer, doing his best to support his large family. Today, I realize my dad felt a lot of pressure and responsibility, although he never shared it. When I questioned an older brother about our dad, he told me that Pa was having a lot of physical pain before he died. Pa had told his brother who had just had back surgery, "I am feeling more pain right now than you are." Why hadn't Dad taken better care of himself and gone to a doctor? I truly do feel that my dad did the best he could with what he had been given. Somehow I feel closer to him at this moment than I ever did while he was alive.

I knew more about my mother's background. My mother was the second oldest of twelve children. Because her mother was sick a lot, my mom took over many of the responsibilities of mothering her younger brothers and sister. Then she married and had twelve children of her own. She blamed herself for my "bad nerves." From her, I heard pity for herself and pity for me.

There were periods of time when I hadn't called my mother, and she would phone me and try to make me feel guilty about neglecting her. With some courage, I came to be able to say, "Mother, I am involved in my own struggle and pain, and I cannot handle yours." So I wouldn't pick up on the guilt, I needed to recall what Father Luger told me about my first responsibility being to my own emotional health, then my responsibility was to my spouse, and then to my children.

Four years ago, two days before Thanksgiving, I came home late from an E.A. meeting. My husband met me at the door and told me, "Your mother is dead." My thoughts raced back to my father's death. Remembering how long I had denied that reality, I wondered how I was going to handle this experience of death. Death is final! There is no going back, no last words I could say. How many people in Emotions Anonymous have experienced this same trauma! This time through E.A., the ability to express my feelings would be in my favor. I repeated the Serenity Prayer that had come to mean so much to me, "God, grant me the serenity to accept the things I cannot change, the courage to change the things I can, and the wisdom to know the difference."

A couple of weeks after her funeral I was visiting with Father Luger. "Thank God your mother was the way she was or you wouldn't be what you are today," he said. It gave me something to think about in my moments of self-pity. If I had gotten all I thought I needed, I would not be who I am now. Today, I would not choose circumstances other than the ones I experienced. Once I faced myself, I found a meaning and value to my life I might never have known. Now that I am more open to life, I can see there is always someone there to give me what I really need, not necessarily what I want, but what I need — if only I am not too proud to reach out.

With my mother's death, I could truly appreciate the power of making amends. Even though I experienced a normal grieving period, my guilt was not that deep. I had dealt to a great degree with my anger and resentments toward her in the last few years of her life, so that love and compassion had already begun to be a part of my life with her before she died. I was grateful that I had begun the Eighth Step before her death came.

With the help of E.A., I got in touch with the resentment I felt toward some of my brothers and sisters who I thought did not accept or understand my illness. A couple of my brothers once asked me, "Why don't you quit taking those pills and have a drink instead?" Drinking is an important way for many members of my family to have a good time. For them, a party would not be a party without liquor. Today, I do not see this behavior as any healthier than all the pills I used to take. I used to feel so different from the rest of the family, but I see now that I was not necessarily that much different from them. I ended up in the hospital when I could no longer find a way to cover up my pain. Today, I believe everyone has some pain to contend with. Sooner or later it will come. Breaking out of my self-centeredness and seeing my family's need to be valued and accepted, helped my resentments leave. Understanding and compassion, instead, took the place of those resentments.

Knowing I am going to write about my relationship with my husband next, I am finding it hard to go on. It is not pleasant for me to look back and remember how I treated him. Because I had so little respect and love for myself, it was impossible to relate to Jim in a healthy way. I was critical and fault finding, and I hung onto resentment. I felt Jim should be responsible for my happiness, but I did not see my responsibility in our relationship.

When I got into E.A. and started to see what I had done to my family because of my illness, guilt overwhelmed me. To get rid of my guilt, I made amends to Jim for my neglect and for being so critical.

Part of making amends is making amends to ourselves, too. I had to come to an understanding of enabling before I could let go of my guilt. I had to realize that my difficulty with my family members was not all my fault.

One night I was listening to Phil Hansen talking about the family illness of alcoholism, and I related it to our situation. A person does not get sick all by herself. There are people around the sick person who perpetuate the illness by *enabling*. Enabling means taking responsibility for the person who is sick. That way the one who is sick doesn't have to take responsibility for herself. Some general ways of enabling are the messages we send to the sick person that say she is helpless and can't take care of herself, so we will do it for her. Another way is to put the person down. Still another is telling the person to stop being the way she is and to use her willpower to change. The enabler means well but simply does not understand he is helping to maintain the illness by his behavior. He needs to take care of himself, and he needs to realize he cannot change or fix the person he is concerned about. He also needs to learn about *tough love* which means not tolerating behavior that is unacceptable, not letting himself be used, and not covering up for the sick person's behavior. I have come to believe that unless each family member gets help, they will all take turns getting sick in some way.

"'The spouse is oftentimes sicker," Rev. Hansen has said, "than the dependent person, simply because he or she puts up with such unacceptable behavior." Jim heard this, too, but it was some years later before he could accept it.

Because Jim did not feel qualified for E.A., he got permission from Al-Anon to pattern a program after their group calling it Em-Anon for spouses, families, and friends of people who had emotional problems. This separate group, however, did not succeed. But many couples are coming to E.A. now, making it possible for them to relate to both sides of the problem. Most go to separate meetings, so that they each have their own identity. When our son, Jim, repeatedly caused us concern by his drug and alcohol use, my husband started to get more involved in E.A. and also started attending Al-Anon. This helped him to open up.

Too much of the time, though, I still felt lonely and guilty. More and more I was sharing my pain with Jim. At first he was defensive and told me I wanted too much, but finally one day his defenses dropped, and he started to admit his pain and loneliness too. This painful day helped us make a decision to see a marriage counselor. "We cannot be our spouse's therapist," he said. "If we are having trouble in a relationship, we need some help from the outside." I saw then that Jim was unable to listen to me, because I was too close. Our sessions with the marriage counselor helped us look at our backgrounds and see why we reacted the way we did. I had already learned many of these things through my growth in E.A. Because I needed to continue accepting my personality, I needed to express the things that were important to me. For me, impression without expression leaves depression. But Jim had not felt the desperation that I had, and he was more content to stay where he was.

We are two different people, and neither of us could or should be like the other. We need to accept our differences and be grateful for them and build on our similarities. Many times since I have been in E.A., Jim and I have argued about feelings being right or wrong. In the last couple of months when I've told Jim I was feeling something that I did not like he would reply, "Feelings are not right or wrong; it is okay for you to feel that way." We look at each other and smile.

Today when I feel someone loves me, I feel that person really cares about me and values me as a person. There is a genuine acceptance of me. That person is also supportive of what I am interested in and is willing to share himself and his interests, too. By recognizing what I appreciate in others, I can work on integrating these things into my own attitudes and behavior. One thing I know for sure, love is not just doing for others. Love is being willing to trust, to let go of the barrier of fear and pride and to share what is really inside of ourselves.

In counseling with Tom, Jim was asked to write down a list of painful experiences he had connected with my illness. When it came time to read his list, Jim told Tom the hardest thing for him to accept was the fact he had accepted unacceptable behavior for so many years. Jim had been brought up to believe in peace at all costs. In a way I had, too, but my stress point was lower than Jim's, so I ended up in the hospital. My body and emotions were saying, "I refuse to handle peace at all costs."

When I first told some of my friends that Jim and I were going for marriage counseling, the response I received from them was, "Don't you think you are looking for too much?" My answer is, "No. Jim and I refuse to live any longer with peace at all costs."

I believe every effort should be made to save a marriage. I also believe many marriages could grow into happy and successful relationships if people really understood the dynamics and stages of marriage. These are realizations I have come to only in the past two years. Marriage often goes through these states: 1. romance, 2. disillusionment, 3. despair, 4. growth, 5. maturing love. Sadly, many people settle in at disillusionment or despair and just exist while others get to this point of disillusionment or despair and think because the romance is gone, the marriage is over, and they want to call it quits. If they split and then go on to a new relationship, this new relationship will eventually lead to the same place. What is not resolved in one relationship will be brought into the next. Sooner or later we need to stay and face ourselves.

In suggesting staying in a marriage, I am not talking about staying in a situation where there is mistreatment or abuse, but in a situation where the main problem is caused by our pride and our fear, and where both people are willing to take responsibility to work through the conflict. It takes a lot of hard work and patience, but I believe the effort put into a relationship by a couple will be rewarded abundantly with feelings of peace, harmony, belonging, and love. In the Program I have heard it said that it is never advisable to make important decisions in the midst of turmoil, resentment, or self-pity. As a criteria, this has worked for me over the past years in dealing with my relationships.

Probably the most painful relationship I have to look back on is the one with my boys. Through their young years, my emotional problems were serious. Because of my repeated trips to the hospital, my depression, and suicidal tendencies, I made life a hell for all of us. I sat down with each of them individually to make amends, telling them I was sorry for the way I had acted and the way I had treated them, and I told them that my illness was not their fault. As I began to grow in the Program, I let them know they were not responsible for my behavior. I tried to remove the guilt they might have felt for my illness. I tried to show them I didn't expect them to be the same and that I appreciated each of them for the person he was. As well as I could, I began allowing the boys to develop their own individual personalities.

Through my process of growing in E.A., I have experienced

both the pain and the joy of learning to love. Really loving my children now is very different from what I used to think love meant. Love is not controlling or manipulating. It is not wanting my children to look good and do the right things so they will reflect well on me. Love is giving them acceptance, encouragement, direction, and eventually freedom so they can grow up being emotionally independent. I can also love by being confrontive, sharing my needs and my values, and not accepting unacceptable behavior. It is certainly not love if I let them use me because of my guilt feelings from the past. In Step Eight, I again see willingness as a key, the willingness to let go of blaming others or ourselves. As long as we are blaming ourselves, we feel guilty. Entertaining these feelings on a constant basis causes us to behave irresponsibly today. The fact is that only I am responsible for my unhappiness or my happiness today.

Willingness to understand and to forgive others is closely connected to understanding and forgiving ourselves. If we want to resume a healthy relationship with those people we feel have harmed us, we need to forgive them. At the same time we need to forgive others even if we don't want to resume a relationship with them. Because our unforgiveness hurts us and cuts us off from experiencing a loving God in our lives, we need to be willing to forgive everyone and, of course, this includes ourselves.

CHAPTER NINE

The answer to guilt — forgiveness

More than any other factor, guilt perpetuated my illness. Some of the guilt was real guilt because I had harmed others, but all too much of my guilt was neurotic guilt arising from setting unrealistic values that no human being could possibly live up to.

Real guilt comes from actual harm we have done to others. We feel alienated from God and from the person we harmed. Trying to rationalize my guilt did not make it go away. My rationalization only buried my guilt, and while it festered inside, it caused me anxiety, panic, depression, insomnia, and suicidal tendencies. I separate neurotic guilt from real guilt. Neurotic guilt came from not living up to a perfectionistic expectation of myself. A couple of feelings that identify neurotic guilt are shame and embarrassment. Because I set unattainable goals for myself, I constantly felt guilty. I had to begin looking at my goals daily, examining their reality. If I saw myself with unrealistic goals in an area, I asked God to help me let go and set up a more human goal for myself. Previously, with the goals I had set, I had denied my humanity. While I was busy feeling guilty for being human, it kept me from doing the things that I could have reasonably expected myself to do. Neurotic guilt uses up a lot of energy.

A definition I especially like of neurotic guilt is that it is a pretense of virtue we never had in the first place. Another way of saying it is, the distance between our real self and the self we want others to see is the amount of guilt we experience.

In an earlier chapter I talked about how guilty I felt when I realized my anger at God. One night Phil Hansen was talking about anger toward God, and he said, "If you are angry at God, it means you have a relationship going. You don't get angry at someone who means nothing to you."

While doing my first Fourth and Fifth Step, many repressed guilts surfaced. There I learned that the only answer to guilt was forgiveness. First, at a conscious level I understood that God had forgiven me, but at a subconscious level I still felt guilty. Finally, the realization came that there was no virtue connected with my guilt and that God did not want me mentally or verbally rehashing my wrongs. He wanted me to let them go and to forgive myself. If we owed a bill at a particular store and paid it in full, would we go back again and again to pay the same debt? If we did, our sanity would be questioned. Yet this was the way I responded to God's saying, "Debt paid in full." Realizing I did not have to go back again and again to God, and that if I did so I would be putting myself above God, I prayed each day, "God, I know You have forgiven me. Help me forgive myself."

Today, if I hang on to guilt, I know it keeps me from being responsible, so I try to deal with it as soon as possible. By talking to someone about my guilt and making amends if it is necessary, I can let the guilt go. For a long time I thought to simply accept myself and to tell myself I had done the best I could with what I knew, and to forgive myself for failing to live up to a reasonable expectation was a copout. The old message rang clear: For the things I had done wrong, I should be punished.

For years when I felt guilt, I unconsciously looked for a way to punish myself. When I had punished myself enough, the guilt left, and then I had the excuse to go back and repeat the same negative behavior. To get rid of guilt, we need to change our behavior and our attitudes. Change is the responsible approach to guilt, not self-punishment. The old programming in the guilt area was stronger than any other for me so over a long period of time, I consciously had to tell myself two things; not forgiving myself was a copout and not forgiving myself was putting myself above God.

In a previous chapter I shared how imperative acceptance, honesty, and willingness are to the success of working this Program. I further believe that until I could finally believe God had forgiven me and I, in turn, could forgive myself, little progress was made. A turning point for me was accepting my

responsibility for the part I had played in the incidents that
happened to me as a child. As small a part as I might have
played, I was there.

This change in attitude helped me let go of the resentment I
had toward those people. My resentment had kept my guilt going
in an unending cycle. Unless I could begin to forgive others for
their mistakes and imperfections, I could not expect to be able to
forgive myself. How relieved I was to realize that no matter how
much I might want to go back and change many of the things that
had happened, I did not have to make up for any of my past
wrongs or failings because God's love had already taken care of
them.

Guilt and punishment had always gone hand in hand. But no
more. If I feel guilty today, I look at its validity and deal with it by
changing my behavior, by making amends, or by accepting my
own humanity. Oftentimes, there is no valid reason for the guilt
feelings I experience except that they were such a strong,
powerful pattern in my life from my youngest years. Just because
I do not think I have reason to feel guilty, I must be careful then
not to deny the presence of guilt. Whatever feeling we stuff
inside controls us while the feeling we bring out in the open loses
control over us. I really believe a statement I once heard, "You
can't use shock treatments to get rid of guilt." Today the answer
to dealing with my guilt, real or neurotic, is sharing it with
someone I trust. (If you are saying there is no one you can trust,
remember, I used that excuse, too.) Sharing my guilt helps me
sort it out.

I know today that not to truly forgive myself is a copout. If we
hang on to guilt consciously or unconsciously, we will need to
find a way to punish ourselves. While punishing ourselves, we
are apt to lash out at those closest to us and also cause them pain.
When we can accept God's forgiveness and then forgive
ourselves, we are free to be a more kind and loving person that
day, not only to ourselves, but also to the other people who are in
our lives.

Earlier I talked about my compulsive behavior surfacing in my
house cleaning and in my outward appearance. A more painful
surfacing of my scrupulosity was in my sexuality, the area of
myself I feared the most. As I am sitting here writing about this

area of my life, I feel tension in my whole body. My old control is wanting to take over and not share this area, but with God's help I will go on.

I dealt with my sexuality, with three different priests who counseled me, their names were Denny, Dick and Arnie. I talked with Denny for about half an hour the first time about how negative I felt about sex and about how guilty it made me feel. He said to me, "Pat, you will never be a whole person until you can accept your sexuality." Those words have come back to me many times and given me the courage to deal with my sexuality. Talking to Denny about sex and getting out the pain and guilt I had felt from my past was just the beginning.

Later, Denny told me to stop telling myself sex was still something to feel guilty about. After I told Denny that I thought my disliking sex was a punishment for getting married, and maybe I was supposed to have become a nun, he laughed and said, "You would have made a hell of a nun with all your scruples." Then I realized that with all my sex hangups I might have ended up doing more harm to some little girls than had been done to me. So I let go of that guilt.

Talking with Dick a few times about sex, I told him, "I wish I had never married, then I would not have to deal with my sexuality." Dick replied, "It should be a lot of fun for you to work on your sexuality." But at that time I didn't find what he said humorous.

Sex was still a topic of discussion with Arnie for a couple of years. Although I had come a long way with accepting my sexuality, I continued to find new areas of discomfort with sex. As I was becoming more free, I would awaken from a dream having sexual feelings. Because they felt good, I did not want to let them go. But I felt guilt for feeling this pleasure because I was taught sexual feelings were to be enjoyed only during intercourse and then only if I wanted to have a child. If I did not want a child, then I was being selfish to enjoy sex. Arnie was so understanding and accepting when he said, "Just accept your sexual feelings. They are a part of your humanity and are okay. Dwelling on them because you feel uncomfortable with them only builds them out of proportion." He let me know quite emphatically that "pleasure is God's invention."

Along with my problems with sexuality, birth control was another area of pain. I had been so indoctrinated against birth control that back in high school, in a public high school, mind you, I had written a theme in my senior year about the evils of birth control. My teacher responded to me saying, "I would like to talk to you when you are an adult and see how you feel then." In my rigidity, I felt there was no way I would ever change my mind.

Well, the reality came. I had two children followed by a breakdown, and the thought of another baby frightened me half to death. I had my hands more than full with what I already had. Not wanting to have another child caused me enormous guilt. In the next few years I had two more breakdowns which increased my feelings of not wanting the added responsibility of another child.

I talked about birth control with Denny, Dick and Arnie, and a few friends. Through their direction I came to realize that for me not to practice birth control would be a copout because at that time I did not enjoy sex, and I was afraid of pregnancy. What better excuse for avoiding intimacy? What kind of a marriage relationship would that be? To expect Jim to stay in a marriage like that would have been more selfish of me than to practice birth control. Although it seemed to come from an unconscious level, every time I wanted to copout from our relationship, I picked up on my old guilt for practicing birth control.

Denny helped some by explaining to me the spirit of the law versus the letter of the law. Explaining the lesser of two evils, he said, "It is not right to kill, but if a person is doing it in self-defense, it would not be wrong. If a woman is going to end up climbing the walls or having a breakdown by having more children, it really seems better to take care of the children she already has."

When I talked to Dick about feeling selfish and guilty because I did not want more children, he laughed at me and said, "Pat, I don't see you as being selfish, just because you don't want more children. Look at the encouragement and support you are willing to give others who are hurting emotionally. Did you ever stop to think that this is where God wants you to spend your time and energy, giving love and support to His children who are already here?" Touched deeply by Dick's understanding and perception, I felt my Higher Power talking through him that day so his words have stayed with me. Another reason I had a hard time handling the birth control issue was that I was led to believe a woman's value was in how many children she had. Coming from a family of twelve, I felt I needed to have at least a half-dozen children to be a worthwhile person. Today, I no longer believe in my old ideas of a woman's worth coming from only having children, and I have finally resolved the birth control controversy. When authority speaks on this subject, I feel comfortable with my own decision and no longer feel intimidated. No one can or will answer to God for my life but me.

In the past couple of years, along with finding beauty in my sexuality, I can enjoy it. Yet it is extremely difficult, if not impossible, to be intimate with my spouse if our relationship is not going well. I need openness, sharing, and a feeling that Jim trusts me in order to be able to handle sex. Otherwise, the old feelings of being used or doing it out of duty or obligation come back. No longer can I tolerate sex with those kinds of feelings.

Often, I have been envious of others who could simply pop into bed to have sex even when their relationship was not going well. Having been open with enough people who have in turn shared with me, I find out their jumping into bed was not that great after all. Then the other day I heard Jess Lair say again something I had heard him say before but had forgotten, "Oftentimes people jump into bed to avoid intimacy." Thinking about my friends' sharing and what Jess said causes me to lose much of my envy. Recently I heard a speaker talking about intimacy. She said something that really hit home. "There can be no intimacy in a dependent relationship."

My neurotic guilt blew many experiences out of proportion. Here again bringing some of these experiences back to the surface causes me tension. In the past when I opened my mind up and let in one neurotic guilt, more were sure to follow. Because this guilt was impossible for me to turn off, I will put my writing about these experiences in God's hands and believe that my mind will stop when I am through sharing.

An example of neurotic guilt was when I was eighteen and going with Jim. We went to his parent's cabin to visit for the day, and their toilet did not flush properly. The top of the commode had to be lifted to move something in the tank to flush it. While lifting the top to flush the toilet, I accidentally cracked it. Being embarrassed and afraid of being rejected, I did not go to Jim or his parents and share this. Eleven years later, having punished myself hundreds of times with this guilt, I sat down with Jim's mother and shared what had happened. The tension and fear built up the day I decided to make amends until I felt I would explode if I did not share it. Tearfully, I described this experience, and Jim's mother told me to forget it because she didn't care about it at all. If I had told her the day it happened, I am sure she would have responded the same. Getting it out got rid of the guilt.

Another experience which caused me repeated pain came a few years after the tornado. A neighbor started kidding me about the perfection I had expected from the contractor and how I had taken advantage of the contractor and the insurance company by getting more than I had coming. Several people told me that there was no way an insurance company or contractor would give me more than I had coming. But every so often this same topic came up, and I hooked into it and felt guilty and wanted to run away from my humanity and back into my symptoms.

One day after being in E.A. about three years I decided I would call the contractor. I did not care if the contractor would respond and say, "Yes, you did take advantage of me, and I want two thousand dollars from you." At that point my sanity was worth a million. As I placed the call, I was scared to death. Luckily (the Grace of God again, I'm sure) the contractor was right there. I told him who I was, why I was calling, and my involvement in E.A. I let him know I had been sick and was sorry for being so demanding and bitchy. His response was not what I expected. He replied, "Everybody was uptight at that time. Forget about it now and take care of yourself. There is no way you could have taken advantage of me or the insurance company." Through my tears I thanked him and hung up the phone as more tears of relief and healing poured out. No more did I need to punish myself with that experience.

Another time I felt I had cheated on a game at a shower, and winning the prize caused me enormous guilt and anxiety. As it ended up, I probably would have won the prize anyway, but I called the gal who gave the shower because I couldn't stand my dishonesty. She was very kind, understanding, and accepting which helped me accept myself a little easier.

Another example was being undercharged for something I had bought. Because I knew I would use this later to punish myself if I did not pay, I called the store and told the clerk so she could charge the extra money I owed to my account. She was surprised and appreciative of my honesty and thanked me for calling.

Still another time, I broke a zipper trying on a skirt and left the store only to get home and feel terrible. So I called the store and told the clerk who was accepting of me, too. She told me this often happened, not to worry about it, and thanked me for calling.

To make peace with myself, except when doing so hurts another person, is a top priority of mine. Today I am grateful for the maturity and acceptance of myself I have gained through the Program. If I do something that bothers me, even if it may seem stupid to someone else, I take care of it right away. No longer do I want to build on that kind of self-destruction. As I deal with the real causes of pain in my life, the neurotic symptoms cause me less problems.

Initially, I felt the step of making amends (Step Nine) was to humiliate me, and I wanted no part of it. After awhile I learned the purpose of making amends is not to humiliate us but to help us make peace with our past and give us freedom to go on in the present. Making amends actually promotes self-worth. Another purpose of this Step is to help us discover the things we use to punish ourselves; things which unrecognized cause us feelings of wanting to retreat with our symptoms, go back to our pills or into the hospital. This awareness was absolutely vital to my continued growth and recovery. Only with this awareness could I choose to take positive action.

In making amends we are not looking for a response or any amends back. Our responsibility is to clean up our side of the relationship. If we go to another person only because we want their acceptance and do not feel we have harmed them, but that they have harmed us, we are being dishonest with ourselves and defeating the purpose of this Step.

Because of my neurotic guilt, I was advised by many people in

E.A. to be careful about my amends. I was careful not to go off in a flurry to rid myself of an uncomfortable feeling and hurt someone else in the process. Each time I would stop and ask myself, "Will I hurt the other person by what I am saying? Will only my pride be hurt?" If I felt resentment or if I had gossiped about another, and they did not realize this, the best amends I could make would be by changing my attitude and by understanding where they were coming from. When I was hurt by a person and retaliated by criticizing them to someone else, I learned that "hurt people hurt people." When I am happy with myself, I do not go about and deliberately hurt someone by my words or actions.

If we want to be forgiven for the harm we have done, then we also need to be willing to forgive another. If we have the right to make a mistake, so do others. As a general guide, if there is someone we may not want to face if we see them somewhere, we need to look and see if we have some amends to make.

I found after making amends that this brought me a clearness in my thinking that then made me able to better understand detaching and enabling. These concepts from A.A. and Al-Anon are vital to healthy relationships. I used to think that to detach meant we could let go of someone we loved immediately and be free of pain. Now I believe detaching is somewhat like surrender. I am able to let go in areas and in degrees, hopefully to arrive at a point where I am not affected by another person's pain or behavior.

Some examples of detaching are:

1. Not denying the existence of a problem.
2. Not covering up or accepting unacceptable behavior.
3. Letting go of thinking about a problem that is destroying my peace of mind.
4. Letting someone I love feel pain without trying to take it away or to fix it up.
5. Not trying to relieve another of the responsibility for his actions.
6. Not letting another person control me by anger, indifference, or pain.
7. Taking all the action I can in a situation and then sitting back and letting the results of it be in God's hands.

8. Confronting someone in a loving way with my concern about their behavior and letting go of the outcome.
9. Letting the person suffer the consequences of his or her own behavior and still standing by with love.

In detaching, we need to take care of our needs by sharing our own pain with someone who understands, and eventually we are able to leave the person we are concerned about in God's care, trusting in His loving guidance, and hoping then to be relieved of our pain. Of course, it is easy to detach when all is going well. The test of detaching is letting go when there is a problem that is causing us pain.

In a sense, enabling is the opposite of detaching. Some examples of enabling are:

1. Denying a problem exists.
2. Ignoring the person I have concern about.
3. Criticizing or putting down.
4. Checking up by watching another's behavior.
5. Taking on another's financial or psychological responsibilities.
6. Helping someone out of a crisis they created, thereby alleviating their pain.
7. Letting someone's behavior control me or my response to them.
8. Stewing about a problem.
9. Trying to fix up, or do too much for another by giving him a feeling of being helpless to care for himself.
10. Reacting verbally to what another person says or taking it personally and withdrawing.
11. Explaining and defending others' actions to myself or others.
12. Letting another project his unhappiness on me and allowing myself to feel guilty.
13. Telling the person I am concerned about to either shape up or use his willpower to change.
14. Using blame, shame, or guilt to control another.
15. Trying to control someone by anger or by being silent.
16. Not being honest and open about my feelings.

To keep from enabling, we need to share in a direct, loving way our concern about another's behavior and how it affects us without attacking that person. If we are paying someone's debts or bailing them out of a difficulty, it is fairly easy for us to see that as enabling. The emotional kind of enabling is more subtle and takes much longer to see. Someone who feels guilty can make a good enabler. I could not see or understand detachment or enabling until I had made amends in my own life.

CHAPTER TEN

Only the disciplined are free

Whenever I used to think of discipline it brought back memories of control imposed from outside. Words that I associated with discipline were: *should, ought, must, have to, right, wrong, sacrifice, denial,* and *punishment.* Needless to say, discipline was not a comforting idea.

Since I have been in E.A., my attitude toward discipline has changed. Discipline no longer comes from outside authority, but comes from within me. This kind of discipline gives me freedom to be, to think, and to grow toward my potential good. With this new perspective, whenever I think of discipline, I sense a feeling of freedom and growth.

No other area is as important to discipline as my thinking. Because I did not know I had a choice in my thinking, my most constant companions were guilt, self-pity, fear and worry. What a revelation to discover that we can choose to change our thinking! I had never realized it before, but the thoughts I constantly dwelled on determined the direction my life had taken. My thinking affected my feelings, my feelings affected my attitudes, and my attitudes affected my behavior. How I behaved formed my feelings about myself and life. This way of responding became a vicious cycle that kept repeating itself.

In the beginning, breaking out of my negative thinking took every bit of effort and energy I had. Because my negative thinking had become so ingrained in my subconscious no matter what experience came along, my first thoughts about any experience were always negative. Minute by minute, I had to consciously replace fear, worry, guilt, and self-pity with something positive. I would use the slogans of E.A. again and again, particularly, "Let Go and Let God."

73

Because my old programming seemed to have more control over me than my positive efforts, I often felt an internal battle. Reminding myself about the enormity of my illness always helped me to see that in spite of my old programming, I could still change today. All I needed was desire to become well, a persistence to change and a willingness to *act as if* the Program would work. Because it had helped so many others, I tried, and the progress that came from my daily efforts kept me from my own self-destruction.

More and more I am finding it is not so much the problems I have experienced that have hurt me and caused me to want to give up and to feel I could not cope, but my reaction to them. By the attitude we hold toward ourselves and life, we create so much of our own happiness or misery. By looking for the good, generally we see good coming to us. When we concentrate on the negative, usually we get more of the same. We get from life just what we think we deserve and what we expect, no more and no less.

Because I used to dislike conflict, I had the idea it was bad. Now I see conflict as healthy. Discussing a problem, although it may be terribly uncomfortable, can bring feelings of relief and self-worth. To avoid the pain of conflict, I used to run from it or ignore it. Avoidance only increased the intensity of my pain and over a long period caused me to lose confidence in myself and my capacity to deal with life.

Conflict usually brings with it feelings of anxiety. Not dealing with the anxiety causes us to feel even more helpless. While experiencing anxiety, we feel the desire to do something as well as our fear of doing it. This awareness helps me to get off the fence and take some action. Once the decision is made or the action is taken, most of the anxiety leaves. Even though there are times I stew and fret about whether the action I have taken is the best, taking action is imperative. I have found that the alternative is being paralyzed with anxiety. By talking with others about what I was feeling and doing, I realized that I had to make a decision. My decision would not always be perfect, and that is where accepting my humanity came in.

Another area causing anxiety was changing my beliefs and values. Change was accompanied by insecurity and doubt, and I did not like this uncertainty. At those times I needed to look back and remember how horrible I felt when I was trying to control my life. Then it became easier for me to be willing to face the challenge of change with its risk and its insecurity. Change was hard to handle, and it took me some time to feel comfortable with my new ideas and beliefs. At first when others did not agree with me, I figured I must be wrong. Eventually, through persistence and support, I developed some inner security to believe that others were entitled to their own beliefs and values, and I was entitled to mine.

In the early years of my growth, the pendulum swung from one extreme to the other. One area of this swing was in recognizing how much I had done for others to gain their approval. For a time I went to the other extreme and did little for others, concentrating on taking care of myself and my own mental and emotional health. Another area of pendulum swing was in my relationship with my boys. Instead of blaming them, I was now constantly blaming myself. After a period of time these areas began to come into more balance.

One night an E.A. member was telling me how it was against her religion to smoke, drink, or dance, even though she knew it said nothing against these activities in scripture. I felt myself reacting. Church laws make God so small! Seeing some rebellion in my reaction, I know I am not completely free from my old programming. I thank God, though, that I am free enough not to believe any longer in a God who is handing out rules and regulations that cause me to feel rigid and fearful. My belief against this concept of God is very strong. I know that my rigid adherence to rules, laws and rituals caused most of my emotional trauma. My rigidity was also a destructive alienation from God.

Seeing reality today is far different for me than it used to be. As I have grown, I see that my symptoms, which were causing me so much pain, were also giving me some payoff. When my symptoms were so exaggerated, they kept me from feeling my terrible isolation, inadequacy, and failure. The biggest payoff of all from my symptoms was not having to be responsible for myself and being able to find others to take care of me. Although this attention was negative, at the time I had perceived it as love — a hell of a substitute for the real thing!

When I used to talk about a problem and someone would reply with some insight for me, I would often say, *Ya, but. Ya, but* meant, "I'm unique. You don't really understand how bad this problem is, I'm in a different situation, and I can't get out, I can't change, I am too young or I am too old, I can't take care of myself, I am too scared." *Ya, but* is an excuse to stay in misery.

Should is another excuse word I watch for. I *should* do this, I *should* feel different, or I *shouldn't* be this way. In the Program I have heard the expression, "Don't *should* on me." Whose *should* am I feeling? How long have I had this *should*? Does it still have relevance today? Did it come from what others told me I *should* do? Or does it come from my own self-expectations? Or from both? *Should* usually produces guilt or inadequacy. A few months ago I heard that *should* means, "I don't want to, so I probably won't." If I hear myself saying, "I should," I replace it with either *I will* or *I won't*. I will or I won't are positive and make me responsible right now.

Can't is another excuse word that goes along with *but* and *should* which I used to keep me from taking responsibility. I *can't* do that really means I *won't*. If I hear myself saying I *can't*, I stop and ask myself *won't* I or *can't* I?

If only my life had been different; *if only* my dad hadn't died; *if only* I hadn't gotten sick. *If only* keeps me living in the past feeling sorry for myself because I did not get what I wanted, and it keeps me from getting my needs met today. *If only* is trying to change something from the past, which, of course, is impossible. If I feel myself thinking, *if only*, I stop myself and follow through with the *if only*. For instance, *if only* my dad hadn't died when I was so young, I might not be afraid of getting close to someone and then losing them. The fact is that my dad did die, but I do not have to be locked into that fear today. The past is gone forever.

What if usually projects something negative into the future. *What if* that happens? *What if* it doesn't work out? *What if*? Along with projecting some disaster into the future, *what if* keeps me in a turmoil and unable to function in a responsible manner in the present. If I catch myself saying *what if*, just being aware that I am saying it can help me to let go of what I am stewing about. I can't do anything about tomorrow until tomorrow comes. Some other ways of making excuses for myself and my misery are rationalizing, minimizing, justifying, and blaming. There was a lot of self-pity and feeling unique in using these excuses.

Because I believed it would help, I did a lot of *thinking* about things only to discover that my intellectualizing kept me from being able to feel. In fact, it was my way of avoiding feelings. "Head tripping" (intellectualizing) kept me from being able to take positive action in the present.

During my first years in the program I heard over and over again that anger and resentment are our number one enemy. When we resent someone, we become their slave. Believing these facts, I wanted no part of being angry or resentful. Although it is true that the anger and resentment that we hang onto are not healthy for us and do us great harm, if we bury these feelings or say, "we shouldn't feel this way any more," we'll really get into trouble because feelings will always come out, either directly or indirectly.

What I now interpret this to mean is that we are not to keep re-feeling the hurt and the pain that causes the anger and resentment. Acknowledge its presence by sharing it with someone, and then be willing to let it go. Saying we shouldn't feel a certain way does us more harm in the long run.

Over these past years I have become aware that behind resentment and anger is a great deal of fear and pain. Resentment and anger come across as power and control kinds of feelings whereas fear and pain come across as helplessness and weak kinds of feelings. My resentment and anger were covering up my pain and my fear. Getting in touch with the pain and fear helped my anger and resentment to dissipate.

Lately I discovered something else about myself while feeling resentful toward my husband. Feeling resentful served to keep me from recognizing and taking responsibility for asking for something I needed. What a revelation! I can get rid of my resentment by looking at what I need and asking for it! Again I had to be aware that it is okay for me to ask for a need to be met. I just needed to become aware of my need and to take the responsibility to ask for it.

Since my discovery that I can get rid of my resentment by looking to see what I need rather than expecting another person to change to meet my needs, I have been listening attentively at meetings when people talk about their resentments. Often, behind their resentment, I hear them wanting to change another to meet their own needs. It has made me realize how much energy I wasted trying to manipulate another to change when I could have quite possibly gotten my needs met by simply asking honestly and directly for it. It is always possible that my request may be denied but that's the risk. My resentment lessens just from the asking.

Self-pity is a powerful tool to control others. In my self-pity I felt I was weak and helpless to change so others should help me out. I never recognized the power I had in my negative state until I saw others coming into the program who were acting helpless. Looking at their helplessness made me realize how much of my God-given power I had used destructively.

When I am full of self-pity, it is impossible for anyone to meet my needs. In this frame of mind, no human being could possibly give me enough. Self-pity turns those closest to me away more quickly than any other emotion I know of. Until I could feel I could gain love in a positive and healthy way, the martyr part of my personality was hard to let go.

Recently on a recorded message from a chemical-dependency unit I heard over my telephone some ideas about feelings that state beautifully what I have come to believe. "Our feelings are our sixth sense, the sense that interprets, directs, arranges, and summarizes our other five. Feelings tell us whether what we are experiencing is painful, threatening, regretful, dull, important, sad or joyous. Feelings can be described in simple and direct ways. There is nothing magical or mystifying about them. When feelings speak, we listen and sometimes respond, even if we do not always understand why. Not to be aware of one's feelings, not to understand, or to know how to express them is worse than being blind, deaf, or paralyzed. Not to feel is not to be alive. More than anything else, feelings make us human, and they make us belong. To build and to maintain any degree of high self-worth, we must learn to identify our feelings and risk sharing our feelings. This contradicts many of our previous learnings and teachings. We have been taught to avoid disclosing so-called bad feelings. There are no right or wrong feelings. There are no good or bad feelings. Feelings are facts. We need to become as open and honest about our feelings as we possibly can because our feelings are our best and most direct way of discovering the real person inside of us."

Many times I thought that I had more pain to deal with than others. This caused me to feel sorry for myself. Finally, realizing that the opposite end of the spectrum of pain is the capacity to experience joy helped me to let go of my self-pity. Instead of experiencing pain as something scary or fearful, I realized now pain is a teacher that lets me feel my need to change. Without recognizing physical pain, we could die quickly of many different diseases. Recognizing our emotional pain can help us take positive action, too.

As I have felt my loneliness, I have reached out for friendship. As I have felt my anger, I have learned to deal with it and started to find some serenity. As I have felt my despair, I have learned to change my attitude, and I have begun to have the ability to experience joy. The intensity of the pain caused by loneliness, anger, hate, and despair are equaled only by the intensity to experience more deeply the comforting feelings of friendship, serenity, love and joy.

In E.A. we talk about the selfishness of the program, which is different from being self-centered. Working the program selfishly by seeing our need for recovery and using the tools of honesty, openmindedness, and willingness is taking the responsible kind of action we need to help us to get well. By each member taking care of themselves, we end up having a great deal to offer to each other. By being selfish and asking for what we need in an honest way, instead of manipulating, we become less self-centered. In this process we move toward becoming more compassionate and caring, not only toward ourselves, but toward others. By being self-centered, I had tried to get my needs met in sneaky, phoney ways, but by being selfish I am being straightforward and honest about my needs.

A desire I had was to get my driver's license. At sixteen I had taken the first step by getting my permit. Over the next seventeen years I renewed my driver's permit over and over again. I talked occasionally about taking the driving test, but never did. In the fall of 1972, after being in E.A. two and a half years, my husband and I were at a gathering one night, and he came down with severe stomach pains. They were so bad that I needed to drive him to the hospital. For the next three days he stayed in the hospital. First I reacted to his getting sick by becoming resentful. It scared me because I was still quite dependent on him. I also reacted to my not being able to drive our car back home from the hospital. I had to call someone to come and get me, so I decided then and there that I was sick and tired of this dependency. If something serious ever happened to Jim, I would be damned if I was going to be asking neighbors to haul me around. Here again, I needed to become sick and tired and angry enough about this dependency to take some positive action. I practiced in earnest, and two months later I took my test and passed — not with flying colors, but I passed. For years I had been so afraid of failing that I had chosen not to even try. Looking back I can say, today, that while I was experiencing the worst of my emotional problems, it was really a blessing in disguise that I did not drive. I would have been a menace on the road.

Getting my license kept me on a natural high for years because it was an outward sign to myself and to others of my growth. During the first year of my driving, I prayed every time I got behind the wheel. To get from one area to another, if it was a far distance and I was driving by myself, I used the idea of taking one block at a time. When I thought about arriving at my destination and having to go through all the traffic, it petrified me. My friend Helen kept telling me that her sister had told her, "The first year of driving is the worst. After that time you'll have gained confidence." Here again the confidence only came after taking the action.

My first adventure out alone was when I drove to the local bank and to the grocery store. As I was coming out of the bank, I saw a man sitting in the car behind me. Because I was insecure about my driving and thought he was watching me, I backed out and cut too sharp. I hit the fender of the car next to me. It was a small dent amounting to less than fifty dollars. Because of my lack of experience, I was embarrassed and scared. I left my phone number with the owner of the car and thought seriously about returning home. Instead, I thought if I give up now, it will be even harder to get behind the wheel again. So with my shakiness and a prayer, I drove on to the grocery store, shopped, and drove home. When I got home, I cried hysterically as I told Jim what had happened. Jim's reaction helped me because he said, "A bent fender is no big deal. The important thing is that no one got hurt." Only my pride! That fender bender was a good lesson for me and helped me to be even more cautious and not to worry if someone was watching me. It was my pride, worrying about looking like a new driver, that had caused the accident.

In my first year of driving my Higher Power worked overtime to protect me from some of the dumb mistakes a new driver makes simply because of lack of experience. Now I have been driving for seven and a half years, and I can hardly believe so many years have passed. In all those years I had a couple of minor scrapes and one accident where someone plowed into the right side of my car. For a long time I felt fearful of cars approaching me on the right side, but as with all fears, not running from them eventually makes the fears lose their intensity. Today, I value being able to drive and rarely do I get into my car and forget to say thanks to my Higher Power for this freedom.

As a young child I had chewed my fingernails down so far that oftentimes my fingers were sore and infected. One time when my boys were little I had chewed my nails down so far I ended up getting an infection all the way up my arm and had to have my arm in a sling. Needless to say, as an adult I was quite embarrassed by the result of my behavior. At times I had tried to stop chewing my nails, but I never persisted.

I thought to mysef, "Why can't I use the idea from the program one day at a time, to stop chewing my fingernails?" I decided I would take two nails, one from each hand, starting with my thumb nails and try to stop. Chewing my nails had become such a habit that I was not even aware of chewing them. Becoming more conscious of my nail chewing, I saw myself chewing them on one hand while I was busy working with my other hand. I invested in a good file because whenever I found a rough edge I needed a file close by to keep from chewing at it. It took persistence and after six months had passed, my fingernails were finally grown out.

Seven years have now passed, and I am happy to say I have not gone back to chewing my nails. Just the other night my friend

Jan commented to me, "You have such pretty hands you could be in a commercial."

Continuing to take inventory in Step Ten is an extension of Step Four. Because I had tended to be so self-critical and analytical, I found it imperative not to turn my new insights *against* myself. Each time I saw something new in myself that I did not like, my immediate reaction was to feel guilty. One day I thought, "Why feel so bad about seeing the defect? It had always been there, and the fact that I can now see it makes it possible, with God's help, for me to change." Actually, I wasn't getting worse; I was just finally seeing my defects. This meant I was coming closer to God because now I was seeing my need for Him in my life.

A good way to take inventory when we are hurting is to practice HALT. Am I *Hungry, Angry, Lonely*, or *Tired*? Taking care of the area I find that is causing my pain helps me see reality in a clearer perspective. I only have this one day to live. Yesterday is gone. Tomorrow is not yet here. Whatever it is I have to cope with, I can handle just for today, with God's help, and the help of people He puts into my life.

Before E.A., admitting I was wrong was nearly impossible for me. Because I already felt such low self-worth, I felt apologizing would have made me look even worse. When I was wrong, I rationalized by thinking, "If they hadn't said this or done that, I would not have acted the way I did, so it is really their fault." After being in E.A. for a few months, I saw my rationalizing for what it was and started to admit when I was wrong. Instead of diminishing my self-worth, this process increased it. Today I have a new perspective on being wrong. Now I realize all human beings make mistakes simply because we are human. I also realize that I needed my mistakes to help point me in a new direction. In fact, the biggest mistake I ever made was in trying to be perfect.

Looking back over these past few years, I realize that some of my negative behavior and attitudes were not so much wrong at that stage of my growth as they were a learned, inadequate way of responding to life. If I respond with some of those negative patterns, knowing what I know today, I know I am wrong or being irresponsible. Once we become aware, we can no longer go back and excuse ourselves, and we end up feeling good about ourselves. With awareness comes responsibility.

Everyone of us gets negative thoughts. In themselves, these negative thoughts do not create a problem. The problem is caused by our dwelling on the thoughts, analyzing them, and rationalizing them. My analyzing and rationalizing was my attempt to get rid of the negative thoughts, but what I didn't realize was that to get rid of the thoughts, I first needed to accept them. We cannot stop the first thought from entering our minds, but we can do something to stop entertaining them.

CHAPTER ELEVEN

Prayer changes me

Recalling where I have come from in my spiritual life, I feel like shouting, "Thank God!" Remembering where I have been has also given me a deeper understanding and acceptance of the person I am today.

While attending a Catholic school, a strong emphasis was placed on memorizing certain prayers word-for-word. Whether or not we understood the prayer didn't seem to be as important as the fact that we had it memorized. It was also stressed that we must say these prayers daily. The attitude I picked up was that as human beings we were basically sinful. Because of our sinfulness, it was advised that we pray to God through the saints since their holiness would make up for our lack. On our own, we were just not quite good enough for God to listen to our prayers.

And so, as an adult, I said my memorized morning prayers, evening prayers, and table prayers faithfully, but with little thought about the meaning. A strong *should* I picked up was always to pray the Act of Contrition (a prayer of forgiveness) with sincerity, especially before falling asleep each night.

Although most of my prayers were memorized words, when I really wanted something desperately, I asked God for it. When I did not receive what I asked for, I begged and pleaded and made promises to God. Even if I didn't receive what I wanted, I still persisted in my prayers.

While a part of me felt rebellious toward this ritualistic way of praying, I stuffed it because I had also been taught that not to pray was a serious sin. I recall the many missed lunch hours I spent in church after my dad's death, praying in earnest for his soul. I tried to pray him into heaven, because I believed he was helpless to do anything for himself. Of course, I never knew if my prayers were quite good enough so my prayers became compulsive. As fear became more and more a basis for my prayer, I became more scrupulous, obsessive, and compulsive. During the later stages of my illness, I often found myself repeating the same prayer over and over because I didn't think I had said it with enough meaning.

It was hard at the beginning to take the time each day to pray as the program suggests, because I doubted it would actually help me. After all, I had prayed in desperation for years. Painfully, I came to the conclusion that I really did not know how to pray. One day during a quiet time alone, I discovered that I had been trying to hide my real thoughts and feelings from God because I was certain He would reject me. On this day, I came to the stark realization that God already knew every thought and feeling I ever had, and He understood me. It was only then that I realized that prayer is talking to God as I would to a trusted friend.

During my first couple of months in the program, I used the simple idea of *acting as if* I believed. At the start of each new day I simply asked God for help to face that day and at the end of that day, I thanked Him for helping me make it through.

After being in the program about three months, I learned the value of some daily meditation books written for Alcoholics Anonymous and Al-Anon. I gradually got into the habit of sitting down each morning to read a couple of these books. The *Guide to the Fourth Step Inventory** listed feelings and attitudes that helped me understand what was going on inside of me. I would close this prayer time by asking for help to face the day. Many times during the first few years in the program, I often needed to stop during the day to ask God's help to see me through just the next five minutes. At the end of those days, I remembered to say a special prayer of thanks.

Ideally, each day I like to start out my prayer with honesty, gratitude, and a hopeful attitude. I sit alone in a quiet place where I will not be disturbed. I relax and take a couple of deep breaths. This puts me into an unhurried state of mind. I ask God to help me to be receptive to what His will might be for this one day. I listen to Him speak through the meditation books written

---

*Published by Hazelden Educational Materials.

for A.A. and Al-Anon. I think about key passages that speak to my heart, believing this is one way of God's reaching out to me.

I have many things to be grateful for. If I can think of at least two (such as the following), I can start my day in a grateful frame of mind. I am grateful . . .

for finding EA.
for my new concept of God and prayer.
for being able to face a day without drugs.
for a good night's sleep.
for freedom from the symptoms that were once overwhelming me.
for losing the fear of God and of people.
for being able to accept God's forgiveness and, in so doing, being able to let go of old guilts.
for the people who give me love and support (mentioning some of them by name).
for learning to be hopeful and to trust.
for the insight and guidance God continues to give me.
for the many moments of peace and serenity.
for seeing a purpose to my life.
for being able to appreciate the beauty in nature.

Daily, I need to pray for faith, patience, and the willingness to let go. When I am worried about a problem, I ask Him to give me guidance about it. When I have a decision to make, I weigh the pros and cons with Him. If someone comes to my mind who is hurting or has a special need, I pray for that person.

I like to close by thanking God for the gift of the new day, and then I turn my will and my life over to His care for another day by saying the Surrender Prayer, "God, I offer myself to Thee, to build with me and do with me what Thou will. Take away my difficulties that victory over them may bear witness to those I would help of Thy power, Thy love, and Thy way of life. May I do Thy will always." This is a prayer on page 63 of *Alcoholics Anonymous.**

Alcoholics Anonymous, published by A.A. World Services Inc., New York, NY. Also available from Hazelden Educational Materials.

As the day goes along, if some tension builds up, I can stop for a moment and be aware again of God's presence and His guidance. Oftentimes the guidance I will get at this point comes from a friend. Making a phone call to share what is going on within me frees me to again surrender the problem that is causing me the tension. In surrendering, I am not giving up, not giving in, but giving over. I believe God speaks to us through all experiences that are positive. We need to take action. Only by risking have I come to have an optimistic outlook on life.

"You are what you think" is so true. When I used to approach God with the idea I was unworthy, I derived feelings of hopelessness and condemnation. Today, I know that this approach is not prayer, but an excuse to hang on to my old behavior.

If I have time to stew about something, I also have the time to be affirmative. Being affirmative is what I consider meditation to be. It puts me in touch with God and His goodness. Focusing on one positive idea relaxes me and helps me to let go of tension. Some affirmative thoughts that I repeatedly use that help me to meditate are:

God loves me just as I am.
God is closer to me than the breath I breathe;
   He *is* the breath I breathe.
God made me for a purpose, and I am of value to Him.
Nothing can separate me from the love of God.
The good I am seeking is seeking me.
God is bigger than my problem, and He is with me right now.
God is God — What I think about Him doesn't change Him; it
   changes me.
I go to meet my good.
God never closes one door without opening another.
God never lets something be taken away without bringing
   something better.
Be still and know that I am with you.
God wants more for me than I want for myself.
God is in every experience.
This is the day which the Lord has made. Let me rejoice and be
   glad in it.

Trust in the Lord and lean not on my own understanding. In
 all my ways acknowledge Him, and He will direct my path.
Listen with my heart, not with my head.
God's love is sustaining me, surrounding me, and guiding me.

I recall reading in A.A.'s *Twelve Steps and Twelve Traditions*** that
"the only scoffers of prayer and meditation are those who have
never tried it," and that "the rewards of prayer and meditation
are emotional balance." Both of these ideas have held true for me.
For my daily effort to take time for prayer and meditation, I have
been richly rewarded. I have made it through situations that
formerly would have put me back into the hospital or back on
drugs. Prayer and meditation help me get out of God's way.

Time after time, as I prayed for guidance or support with a
particular problem, God sent people into my life. I didn't want
people, I wanted a miracle. I once told Jess Lair that something I
had read caused me to feel I was to rely on God and not on
people. His response was, "Because you are afraid of people, you
chose to interpret what you read in that way."

When I prayed to God, I had to put down my hope that He
would come out of the clouds to work a miracle. People are His
miracle in my life. People were close at hand, but I had to reach
out. If I had continued with my fear and refused to reach out to
people, I would be dead or in an institution. For a time I became
dependent on several people and put them on pedestals. Then I
realized that putting people on pedestals was still another way of
running from them. I can't take people out of the picture and try
to do it alone with God, because God so often works through
people.

I went through a painful experience when a neighbor of mine
who was in the E.A. program took her life. It frightened me,
because I was still not so sure I wouldn't do the same thing. My
belief in God seemed to waver and disappear. Panic returned,
and I felt terribly alone. Around four a.m. one morning I
suddenly awoke with the thought, "Disbelief in God is anger for
not getting my own way." How true it was! I was really angry

**Twelve Steps and Twelve Traditions*, published by A.A. World Services
Inc., New York, NY. Also available from Hazelden Educational
Materials.

about her death. That insight has stayed with me, and since that time I have had few times of doubt or disbelief in God's existence, His love, or His care. Often I have heard it said, "If God seems distant, who moved?"

When we want God's help, we need to be honest with where we are because that is where He meets us. If my house is on 57th Avenue, and I keep going to look for it on 59th Avenue because I want it to be there, I certainly will not find it. If I want to continue to pretend my house is on 59th Avenue, and it is the middle of winter, I might freeze to death unless I admit the real location of my house. If I want shelter, I had better go there.

Through an inspiring book, *The Will of God** by Leslie Weatherhead, I learned some ideas about God's will that have helped me again and again. With these new perceptions I was able to begin discarding my old beliefs.

He divided God's will into three categories:

1. God's intentional will.
2. God's circumstantial will.
3. God's ultimate will.

I used to think everything that happened to me and around me was God's will. So naturally, I believed God's will for me was my illness. A few months into the program I had the realization, "How can it be God's will to be both well and sick?"

I have come to believe that God's aim for our life is to be well, happy and productive. God has given human beings a free will and through our free will situations occur that interrupt the good which God intended. Even though the good God wills for us is often interrupted, in the end His love cannot be defeated. He is able to use the most painful and negative events of our life to bring forth good, and through them we can be one with Him.

Something else that I value very much and continue to use is this: if my initial response feels right and the experience is something that will increase my self-esteem, I believe it is God's will for me to do what I feel I need to do. This reminds me that without God's help, I can accomplish nothing of value. This helps to keep me humble so when the outcome is good, I don't take all

---

*Abingdon Press. Nashville, NY.

the credit. I don't deserve it, and it would certainly hurt me to do so.

I believe God wants me to continue taking care of myself and my needs. I take care of my needs daily by using the tools that this program offers me, along with being receptive to other avenues of growth. There is nothing that could ever replace the Twelve Steps, they are my basis for living, and whatever openness or receptivity I have to any new learning has initially come from E.A. experience. Since I have been in Emotions Anonymous, I have also learned many valuable insights from other counseling, workshops, speakers, and books. It never ceases to amaze me that there are new avenues of growth continually being made available to me.

I need the power to carry out God's will when I need to stay with a decision I have made, even if it might be tough for the people-pleasing side of me to do so. I need the power to carry out God's will when I lack faith and trust in the outcome of the situation. I need the power to carry out God's will when I need the courage to stay with a commitment that might result in still more responsibility for me. I need the power to carry out God's will as I see my need to continue risking and meeting new challenges.

It seems to me that the power of God's will is summed up in the ideas contained in the Serenity Prayer. Serenity means, to me, to try to live today with an attitude of tranquility and peacefulness, trusting in God's care. Courage means to live with an attitude of firmness and calmness, forging ahead even when I may be afraid. How often I have been reassured by recalling, "Courage is fear that has said its prayers." Wisdom means to live by using my common sense, making practical judgments, making wise decisions based on my new learning and knowledge.

Through the process of gaining some serenity, courage, and wisdom, we can become more loving, open, and useful human beings. Ultimately, I believe this is what God's will is for us. It seems appropriate for me to close this chapter with a little story that touched my heart.

One night I dreamed I was walking along the beach with God. Many scenes from my life flashed before me. In each scene I noticed my footprints in the sand. Sometimes there were two sets of footprints while at other times there was only one. This disturbed me because it seemed during the low times of my life when I was suffering from sorrow, grief, and despair I could only see the one set of footprints. So I said, "God, You promised to walk with me always, but I noticed that during the most painful times in my life there was only one set of footprints in the sand. When I needed You most, why were You not walking with me?" God replied, "My child, the times that you saw only one set of footprints, I was carrying you."

Chapter Twelve

"I am responsible"

In the later stages of my illness, not a day went by that I did not say, "God help me. God please work a miracle in my life." Before E.A., I believed God used His power magically or mystically to change peoples' lives. Today, I see how unrealistic I was to not realize the commitment that those who were healed must have made and the pain they surely encountered as they continued to grow. Now, I see that a spiritual awakening is the same as a miracle.

Over these past years I have experienced many spiritual awakenings. The miracle of this program working in my life did not come overnight, but I did not get sick overnight either. Growth that comes quickly leaves us when we hit a crisis, while growth that comes slowly sustains us in a crisis. I was told, "Growth is not all forward. It is three steps forward and two steps backward, and sometimes it seems like it is the reverse. Don't give up. You have the tools now. We have been able to make it, and so can you."

One of my more recent spiritual awakenings was my change of heart about having an animal in our house. Having been brought up on a farm, I believed animals belonged outside. Ray and Helen's dog had pups. My son, Tom, expected we would take one of the pups. When Tom asked, I said, "No." There were four pups, and they were ready to leave their mother. Three of the four were spoken for, and Tom came back and asked again. I still said, "No." Then I remembered my friend Mary Jane telling me that her mother would never let her have a pet when she was growing up. Now that her mother was older and alone, she had gotten herself a dog. I thought, "Oh God, maybe I'll get old and senile some day and want a dog, and then the boys will resent

me for not letting them have one." So I sat down with my
husband, and we talked about it. We decided if Tom wanted a
dog badly enough to be willing to pay for its shots and veterinary
visits, we would pay for the food and let him have a dog. We told
Tom what we were thinking, and he was more than willing to
take this responsibility. Before I could change my mind he raced
over to Ray and Helen's to tell them his good news. They
immediately gave Tom the pup because they, too, realized I
might change my mind. My husband and Tom built a wooden
box for the dog to sleep in, carpeted one side of it, and then Tom
brought Brutus home.

The first couple of days we had Brutus I was in a turmoil. I
really did not think I liked animals. I did not want the
responsibility of this animal, yet I felt responsible. I was in tears,
thinking, "I don't want to cope with Brutus, yet if I say the dog
has to go now, the boys will really resent me." I felt damned if I
did and damned if I didn't. So I went to Tom, tearfully, and told
him how I was feeling, and he said, "Mom, when you hear
Brutus, wake me up, and I'll take care of him." By telling Tom and
being assured that he would take responsibility, I thought maybe
I could handle it.

Brutus trained quite quickly and easily. He was allowed only in
the kitchen and downstairs, and he seemed to know his limits.
But my son Jim's bedroom was off the kitchen, and he would
coax Brutus to come into his room. For awhile, I fussed, and then
I relented. Well, if Jim could have Brutus in his, it didn't seem fair
that Tom could not have him in his room too. So it went. Now
would you believe each morning as I wrote this book, Brutus lay
beside me on a blanket on the davenport? I would never have
believed I could have become so attached to an animal. Brutus
has become a member of our family and is loved by all.

The admission fee to this program is a lot of pain. Without my
pain, would I have become willing to change? Would I have been
willing to let go of my egotism, surrender my will, become
honest, be willing to make amends, or to carry the message to
others who were still hurting? I honestly doubt it. I believe that is
why I still need some pain. Without pain, I could cease to see my
need to continue to grow. I might become rigid, narrow, and
self-righteous again.

It is a fact that I spent most of my life trying to avoid pain. I was continually looking for an easier, softer way. In my early years in the program, by trying to avoid pain, I often found myself not wanting to use some of the steps. I was still wanting to find an easier way. Last year I had a most wonderful awakening. Practicing this program *is* the easier, softer way, for it has been the only avenue of help that has given me what I have always been searching for, the security of being loved and belonging.

A few years ago a really rewarding thing happened to me. My son Tom told me he wanted to talk to me, and I dropped what I was doing to listen to him. He said, "Mom, you are really changed." I said hesitantly, "Really, in what way?" He answered, "You are more loving." I was overwhelmed and replied, "Tom, you know what? I feel more loving. I feel like I am just beginning to understand what love is all about."

Sure, I had to work hard to become honest and responsible and have commitment to gain this love and security that I was experiencing, but it was a small price to pay when I look back at the alternative.

Unless people are open to their own feelings, they are not comfortable when others share theirs. When I am involved for several hours with people at a superficial level, or with people using chemicals, I feel lonely again. I can handle it for awhile, but I don't want that involvement on a daily basis. I suppose I am much like the alcoholic who needs to be with other people who also see their need for change. If an alcoholic continues going around with old drinking friends, eventually he may find himself drinking again.

I was also continually searching for happiness. If I got this, or I got that, or if someone did this or gave me that, then I would be happy. Looking for things or people to make me happy simply did not work. Often when I got something I desired, I still was not happy. Happiness was always off in the future. Learning to be happy is a state of mind. I can see now why I was so miserable. Happiness comes from appreciating what we have, not from getting what we think we want. Even more surprising, additional happiness started to come to me as I was becoming honest and responsible for myself. To me, happiness is much like self-worth, a byproduct of taking care of ourselves in an open and honest fashion.

I have discovered that every human being has a tremendous amount of power. That is why it is so hard for some of us powerful people to admit and accept that we are powerless in Step One. When I acted so helpless, I used my power in a negative way, and it made me sick. Getting my power in line with God's will for me has been a slow and sometimes faltering process. I have come to see that the person who sees him or herself in a helpless way, without power, is often manifesting more power than the individual who is open and sees the power he might have in another person's life. If someone is close to us and loves us, it may be hard for them to see our helplessness as power. The power that is more readily seen is the power that is obvious. When I was acting helpless, it was almost impossible for someone who really cared about me not to try to help me. There was a lot of control in acting helpless. Because I have been on both sides of this spectrum, I can often see how I misused power by watching others.

Believing I would never function without my pills, I was quite elated and grateful when two months after I discovered that pills were not the answer to my happiness, I was completely off all of my prescription drugs. At this point I had been in the program for about six months. Instead of reaching for my pills for a quick fix, I was now starting to reach out to people. It was so much more helpful and rewarding.

In my early years in E.A., I was led to believe that my addiction to my pills came from psychological need rather than from a physical need. I thought having a physical addiction was worse. But as time went on, I came to see it did not really make much difference. Any dependency that keeps us from facing ourselves, whether it is alcohol, prescription drugs, street drugs, food, work, power, taking care of others, depression, anxiety, people, or a good thing overdone, can be just as destructive. Alcoholics are not the only people who die prematurely from physical symptoms like liver damage, heart disease, suicide, car accidents, heart attacks or other emotionally-induced illnesses. There are many published statistics that state how much our emotions are involved in the causes of physical illness. If a person is killing himself, what does it matter how? I believe it is important for me to look at myself to see the ways I choose to destroy myself and to not concentrate on other people's problems.

Many times over these past few years I have been aware that there is a type of destruction that occurs in the families of emotionally ill people that is similar to that which occurs in the families of chemically dependent individuals. This was brought home to me when the husband of an E.A. friend tried to take his life last summer and was rushed to the hospital. All of his family were at home that day and saw him carried out on a stretcher and heard the siren whine as the ambulance roared off to the hospital. Just imagine how they felt. What kind of effect did it leave? A lot of hurt, fear, and anger that only time will heal. At least his wife was in the program so she had support from friends. Her experiences in E.A. certainly lessened her feelings of guilt and failure.

Thank God, he did pull through. Because of his suicide attempt, the doctor wanted to give him shock treatments. He did not want these treatments, and his wife did not want them for him either. She and I talked to the psychiatrist about E.A. and shared some of our experiences and the help that we had received. We suggested that this could be a type of support that could really help him. Because her husband wanted to go to E.A. too, the doctor gave him a pass to leave the hospital several nights a week to attend meetings. It was a beginning that gave him support. Now they are both attending E.A., as well as marriage counseling.

I have a dream that some day there will be treatment centers for those with emotional problems patterned after the treatment for the chemically dependent. The support I see in chemical dependency treatment gives the dependent person and the family a way of facing their pain and dealing with it. This dream includes help for the family. I could have benefited from this kind of initial support during my hospitalizations. Not only does the dependent person need help to deal with his pain, the family needs help as well. It is impossible for family members to live with us and love us without feeling pain as they watch us head toward self-destruction. Besides, when we are hurting, we usually lash out and hurt those closest to us. What are our loved ones supposed to do with their pain?

A sadness I feel for the present treatment of the emotionally ill is that in most hospitals they still tend to treat us like we are fragile. Thinking we are fragile, they do not confront us with reality. This keeps us from dealing with our pain. They may even continue trying to take away our pain by giving us pills or, even worse, shock treatments. This only adds to the feelings that we already have that we cannot cope or that we are helpless. I think this approach is outdated.

I believe that any one of us, no matter how fragile we might try to appear in our efforts to control, could cope with the kind of tough love that the chemically dependent person receives in treatment. When someone believes in us, supports us, and lets us know how we can be responsible, we can accomplish what formerly may have seemed impossible.

Another disappointment I have is that emotional illness is still not looked upon by many professionals as a family illness. Focusing only on the member of the family who has broken down causes feelings of loneliness and isolation to continue, not only for the person who collapsed, but for the rest of the family as well. A discovery I have made through some of my A.A. friends and my own son's chemical addiction is that once a person on chemicals stops using, he and his family are still faced with living problems.

It has taken many years for the treatment of the chemically dependent person and the family to be established. I believe this type of treatment could be a beneficial model to help all other types of family dysfunctions, and I believe that in God's time a similar kind of program will be established to the benefit of everyone.

Not too many months after getting into the program, I started to carry the message, because I believe, "I am responsible. Whenever anyone anywhere reaches out for help, I want the hand of E.A. always to be there. And for that; I am responsible."* This quote appears monthly in the A.A. publication called the

---

*The Responsibility Declaration, reprinted for adaptation with permission of A.A. World Services, Inc.

GRAPEVINE**. I substituted only one word by putting E.A. instead of A.A. I am responsible to carry the message of hope to others, but I am not responsible for the results. Phil Hansen puts it cleverly by saying, "We are in sales — not management." In those early days of carrying the message, if someone shared a hurt or a pain, I literally bombarded them with the help I had received through E.A. I wanted everyone to get this wonderful message of hope. It was around this time I heard, "E.A. is not for those who *need* it, it is for those who *want* it." So I became a little more discreet about offering this program to others.

In our local area we have a twenty-four hour answering service for E.A. I became involved and started receiving calls in my home. At first I was scared because I did not know if I could help. But I kept hearing, "We do not give advice on personal or family problems," and "All we have to offer to the newcomer is our story of hope." On days when I was struggling to keep my head above water, I would receive a call and think, "God, help me to say the right thing to this person because I feel so inadequate." Without giving this support and encouragement to others I would not have been able to continue growing myself. A central core of all the Twelve Step Programs is that "in order to keep it, we have to be willing to give it away."

I became involved with carrying the message by speaking to various groups which had requested to hear about our program. The first time I drove to speak after I got my driver's license was to an area that was completely strange to me. I was to meet another E.A. member and go on to talk at a school. With explicit directions, I found my way to the school. Upon arriving I felt relieved. We talked to three classes that day, and it was an extremely rewarding experience. I headed home, took a wrong turn, and ended up in the bordering state of Wisconsin. Realizing I was going in the wrong direction, I turned around, stopped at a gas station to get directions, and headed home again. After arriving home near the supper hour, I realized just how tense I had become. I was emotionally exhausted, but I felt grateful for arriving home safely and for the feelings of accomplishment.

About a month after I received my driver's license, another

**The Grapevine, Inc., Grand Central Station, New York, NY 10163

E.A. member and I were asked to speak to a group of professionals. That morning just happened to be the first snowfall of the season. I made up my mind I was not going to be a seasonal driver. I drove across town to her home, and we went on to speak. It was an exciting experience and one of the first times I could say to myself, "Hey, you guys may have all of your degrees, but I have something to offer just by being me." They responded favorably that day, and I went home flying high. Talking to Ray and Helen that night about the experience, Ray kidded me about my driving in the first snowfall saying, "You were too dumb to know how slippery it was." But I could have cared less about his comments, because I knew my risk-taking in both the driving and talking to that group was a real milestone for me.

Another really special experience of carrying the message was when I was asked to speak by a priest I had confided in during all those years I was so sick. He was now the spiritual director of a seminary, and he wanted me to share my spiritual progress with some seminary students. Just having been asked by him was a touching compliment. After I shared that day, the students responded with warmth and with many questions. I recall one response I made, "I feel as much of a commitment to E.A. as you do to becoming priests. This is because I feel God has revealed himself to me through this program."

This reminds me of a story I heard several years ago about commitment. A pig and a chicken were walking down the street and passed a restaurant. A sign in the window said, "Ham and eggs, $1.25." The chicken turned to the pig and said, "Isn't it wonderful what we do for society and at such a low price?" The pig replied to the chicken, "Yes. But for me it is a total commitment; for you it is only a donation."

Knowing and accepting that I am a dependent person, I realize I need to keep the total commitment of the pig. Only by continuing to take care of myself and by being willing to give what I have received will I keep headed toward the good that is available to me. There are many people who have come into the program and my life and have gone again. The important point is that I am still here, and that I am continuing to grow through my practice of the Twelve Steps.

Another exciting experience was carrying the E.A. message to my former psychiatrist, now head of staff at a local hospital. Along with a couple of other E.A. members, I talked to the doctor and his staff. Because he was open to E.A., we started a weekly orientation of E.A. for the psychiatric patients in this hospital. Only because this orientation series started two weeks after I passed my driver's test was I able to make this weekly commitment. I could see my Higher Power's hand again. This orientation went on for six months and from that orientation a new E.A. group evolved in the hospital.

Starting the hospital group was a growing, challenging, and exciting experience. When patients were open to hearing about E.A., it felt gratifying. On the other hand, when they were closed to E.A., I also felt grateful. They reminded me of where I had been not so long before.

After a year and a half had gone by, and I was not seeing many of the same people returning, I began to question whether my commitment to the hospital group was centered only around ego. Did God actually want me to stay with this commitment? I said to God, "If some commitment from others does not come in these next two months, that will be a message to me that I should give up on this group and go on to something else." The next two months were unbelievable in the growth that I could see taking place. Several members kept coming back, and I could see more commitment. I knew my prayer had been answered. A couple of years later the group had become so large we were breaking up into three groups. Eventually, some of the members left and started other E.A. groups in neighboring communities, which made the program available to still more people. Two years later, we are seeing a need to split again as the group continues to grow.

I believe that family members are the hardest for us to reach. I feel sad when I see them in pain, knowing what they could have if only they made a commitment. It is relatively easy to let them go, for I realize that I am only responsible for carrying the message, the results belong to them and God. I can only pray that some day God will give them the desire for help and put someone into their lives to give them the hope and encouragement that I received.

In my early years in the program, when I read the part of Step Twelve that said "to practice these principles in all my affairs," I got the old feeling of having to do it perfectly. I rationalized that because I have all the tools now, there is no excuse for my imperfections. Needless to say, that kind of attitude had me feeling guilty again. No matter how hard I tried, I found myself falling short.

Over these past years, my idea of practicing these principles in all my affairs has changed considerably. It no longer means to me that we cannot make a mistake or that we cannot fail. But it does mean that when we do fail or make a mistake we take responsibility for it, pick ourselves up, and start over again. Trying to be perfect is what got most of us into trouble in the first place. This program does not say anywhere that we are to become perfect. The program's only goal is to help us become more accepting of our humanity and, in that process, to become more the person God created us to be. To achieve that goal, these are some of the principles we need to practice: admitting, accepting, surrendering, listening, risking, trusting, sharing, commitment, honesty, open-mindedness, willingness, discipline, action, forgiveness, responsibility, persistance, and gratitude.

In my early E.A. days when I was expecting to get nothing back, it was hard to keep on. Often when I felt hurt, I crawled into my shell and thought, "I am not going to open myself to you or listen to you any more." I would stay that way for a few hours. Then I would realize how miserable I was because I was refusing to love. Because I knew a better way now, I realized that closing myself off was only more painful.

I wanted to feel love from others, but first I had to develop the capacity to love myself. I wanted to have strength, but first I had to become willing to carry my daily responsibilities. I wanted to have wisdom, but first I had to become willing to be honest.

While working on this book for the past year and a half, I have felt more gratitude and joy than I had ever thought was possible. I want to say to you that if my story gives you any insight, hope, or encouragement, I am an instrument of God which may help you realize that you, too, have God-given talents and abilities within, something that will meet your deepest need for meaning and purpose; the reason for which you were created.

I would like to close with something that I heard from Gert, the little old gal I mentioned in Chapter Three, who was such an inspiration and expression of God's love and power to me.

"I ain't what I wanna be, I ain't what I'm gonna be, but thank God, I ain't what I used to be."